MINING YOUR CLIENT'S METAPHORS

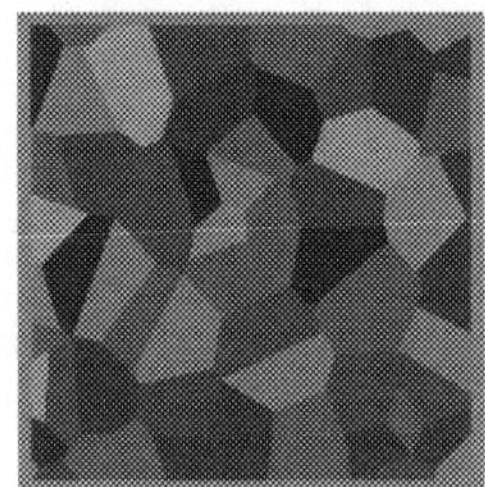

MINING YOUR CLIENT'S METAPHORS

A How-to Workbook on Clean Language and Symbolic Modeling

BASICS PART TWO: FACILITATING CHANGE

Gina Campbell

BALBOA.PRESS
A DIVISION OF HAY HOUSE

Published by Mining Your Metaphors, LLC
Book layout design and typesetting by M. L. Parks
Cover design by Kendall Ludwig

Balboa Press books may be ordered through booksellers or by contacting:

Balboa Press
A Division of Hay House
1663 Liberty Drive
Bloomington, IN 47403
www.balboapress.com
844-682-1282

ISBN: 978-1-4525-7105-8 (sc)
ISBN: 978-1-4525-7106-5 (e)

Print information available on the last page.

Balboa Press rev. date: 11/11/2021

BIRD'S EYE VIEW

How-To Workbooks
BASICS: PARTS I and II

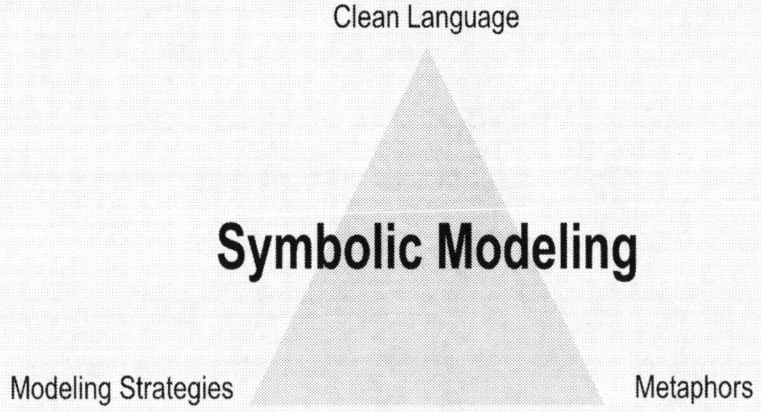

Clean Language

Symbolic Modeling

Modeling Strategies

Metaphors

BASICS PART I: Facilitating Clarity

9 Clean Language Questions about:
- Attributes
- Getting a Metaphor
- Desired Outcomes
- Location
- Time and Sequence
- Relationship

What is Clean Language?
What is Symbolic Modeling?
Structuring a Session start to finish
Facilitation Techniques
Clean Space experience
Working from a Metaphor Map/Drawing

BASICS PART II: **Facilitating Change**

3+ Clean Language Questions about:
- **Conditions for Change**
- **Maturing a Change**

20 Specialized Questions
Creating Your Own Specialized CLQs

The Five-Stage Process
Enriching Part I material
Modeling Strategy
Scope of Practice: Counseling and Coaching

Also by Gina Campbell

Mining Your Client's Metaphors: A How-To Workbook on Clean Language and Symbolic Modeling, Basics Part One: Facilitating Clarity

Panning for Your Client's Gold: 12 Lean Clean Language Processes

Hope in a Corner of My Heart: a healing journey through the dream-logical world of inner metaphors

Acknowledgments

As with the first workbook of this pair, I greatly appreciate the careful review and helpful suggestions offered by James Lawley and Penny Tompkins, the developers of Symbolic Modeling. Thanks also to Eleanor Haspel-Portner, Chaddie Hughes, Jill Rowan, Rosemary Scavullo-Flickinger, Johannes Walker, Zaba Walker, and Brett Welch for their feedback and contributions. I thank my trainees and my clients, who have provided inspiration and taught me well. Finally, I want to acknowledge the late David Grove, whose work with metaphors and Clean Language was the start of this all.

Welcome Back

So, you are ready for *Basics Part Two: Facilitating Change*? Terrific!

I am anticipating that some readers of this book will have just finished *Basics Part One: Facilitating Clarity* and be moving right on to *Basics Part Two* and the next phase of learning how to facilitate using David Grove's ground-breaking technique Clean Language (CL) and James Lawley and Penny Tompkins' Symbolic Modeling (SyM). If so, get ready for new questions and strategies that will widen and deepen what you can do with metaphors.

Others of you will be coming to *Basics Part Two* after a break, during which time I hope you have been putting the skills you learned in *Basics Part One* into practice. But if it has been awhile since you worked with the Clean Language questions, you may feel a bit rusty. I encourage you to go back and at least reread the text portions of *Basics Part One* and practice getting comfortable again with the basic questions. Adding new information, concepts, and Clean Language questions on top of a shaky foundation is not likely to be helpful. On the other hand, some people like to have a concept of the whole process before they dig in to really master the skills. If this is how you learn best, then on we go.

As with any other rich and complex skill, your mastery of Clean Language will come with practice, reflection, and more practice. The more you do it, the more some skills will become automatic, and the more attention you will have to notice what else there is to notice. The more you do it, the more experience you will have to guide your strategy for the next time, as you learn from what worked best.

If you are using this text for a self-study course, I encourage you to find a practice buddy if at all possible. Not only is it far better to actually work with a client, but the opportunity to be a client yourself will hugely inform your own facilitating. And, as you delve more deeply into the strategy of Symbolic Modeling, having a buddy to discuss what you notice, which questions you consider, and which you ultimately choose will greatly enrich your learning. And, it's great fun!

Give yourself permission to be a novice, to be a bit uncomfortable at first, to make mistakes, to take chances and see what happens. Perfection is not required for wondrous things to happen.

Gina Campbell
Director and Trainer
Mining Your Metaphors

Contents

About This Book

If you haven't already, take a moment to look over the Bird's Eye View and the Contents to get a feel for what we will cover in *Basics Part Two*. You may be wondering...

How will what I learn here help me to help my client change?

A client rarely seeks help from a professional because they have a problem; they seek help because they have tried again and again to solve a problem, and their efforts have not been successful. Sometimes just getting really clear about what they want and what resources they have will be all your client needs. Other times, that is not enough. It is about those times that this workbook offers you basic Clean Language Questions (CLQs) and Symbolic Modeling (SyM) strategies to help you help your client. With the skills you will learn, you will be able to offer your client mind/body experiences to access their inner wisdom about:

- **Who they are**
- **What they want or need to change**
- **How that change needs to unfold for the shifts to be comprehensive and lasting**

When it comes to change, enabling your client to experientially engage with their subconscious wisdom through their metaphors can be the key to transformation, whether it is a physical, mental, emotional, behavioral, relationship, organizational, or any other sort of desired change. If that sounds very general, it is because CL and SyM are very flexible tools, which can be used to address most any issue that involves your client's conscious and subconscious minds. You play a vital role as witness and tour guide to your client's profoundly personal and unique inner exploration. The detailed picture that emerges will reveal:

- **Inner strengths and resources**
- **Core beliefs and patterns**
- **Relevant conflicts and blocks**
- **Misconceptions and maladaptive solutions**

With access to these, you can help your client fashion for themselves a more helpful, healthy way of being in the world while:

- **Limiting the extent to which your personal issues, perspectives, biases, and assumptions influence your client's determination of what they want and need**
- **Fostering your client's sense of being truly seen, heard, and respected**
- **Enhancing your client's self-awareness and self-development skills**
- **Working at your client's pace and readiness for change**
- **Strengthening your connection with your client**

CO-CREATING THIS TEXT

You will find numerous places in this workbook where you will be invited to add your answers and record your observations and questions. You can track your progress and mindfully identify which skills you want to hone. I encourage you to take the time to slow down and fill in all the spaces provided for you, taking an active role in creating a text that is tailor-made for you.

Section One

"A large part of self-understanding is the search for appropriate personal metaphors that make sense of our lives."

-George Lakoff and Mark Johnson

Overview: The Five Stages of the Symbolic Modeling Process

In the first workbook *Basics Part One*, you learned how to structure a session from start to finish, from situating to wrapping up. You learned some specific facilitating techniques and equipped yourself with 9 Clean Language Questions and the P/R/O modeling strategy. You attuned your ears to metaphors and resources, and you learned to be wary of your client's explanations. You practiced how to *stay clean,* guiding your client's process while staying out of their content. And you learned to question your assumptions. You are well-equipped for the next leg of our journey into your client's inner world!

The Symbolic Modeling Framework for Change process, as conceived by James Lawley and Penny Tompkins, consists of the five stages described below. You will recognize Stages 1-3 from *Basics Part One*. Mastering Stages 4 and 5 will enable you to meet the challenges for which your practice with clients has likely primed you. Follow along with this next example that illustrates the basic conceptual structure of a Symbolic Modeling session. (Note: I've limited my repetitions of my client's words in places to keep this concise.)

1. *Entering the Symbolic Domain:* As their attention shifts from everyday experiences to their symbolic world, clients naturally ease into a mindful, inner-focused trance state where their conscious and subconscious minds communicate through metaphor.

   Example:

   Facilitator: And what would you like to have happen?

   Client: I'd like to feel more joy in my life. I just don't feel excitement for much.

   Facilitator: And you'd like to feel more joy in your life. And when feel more joy in your life, that's joy like what?

   Client: It's like everything is gray now. I'd like everything to be in technicolor!

2. *Developing the Symbols:* By identifying the metaphors' attributes and locations in their metaphoric landscape, your client learns more about their metaphors and their own inner world.

   Example continued:

   Facilitator: And you'd like everything to be in technicolor! And when technicolor, is there anything else about that technicolor?

   Client: Yes. It's really vivid, lots of reds and blues. Some greens over there. (points to the right)

   Facilitator: And vivid, reds and blues. And greens over there. (points to same place) And when greens, what kind of greens are those greens?

   Client: Oh, now I see—it's long grass.

3. *Creating a Model:* As information about their multiple metaphors unfolds, your client learns more about how they interact with one another. New symbols, problems, and desired outcomes may also emerge, multiplying the interactive elements in your client's metaphor landscape.

Example continued:

Facilitator: And long grass. And is there anything else about that long grass?

Client: Yes, there's…it looks like a path.

Facilitator: And when there's long grass and a path, then what happens?

Client: I'd like to walk on that path and see where it goes. But I can't. The grass is too long; it's hard to walk. *I get too tired. Now, I'm in black and white again.*

4. *Getting Ready for Change:* If your client's desired change does not occur spontaneously as they uncover new information in Stage 3, move on to Stage 4. Your client discovers what conditions need to be met in order for their desired changes to occur.

Example continued:

Facilitator: And you're in black and white again. And when in black and white, what would you like to have happen?

Client: *It's like I'm a camera in black and white mode. I want to be in color mode.*

Facilitator: And you want to be in color mode. And when color mode, what needs to happen for you to be in color mode?

Client: *There's a switch to push to make it color mode.*

Facilitator: And a switch. And when a switch, whereabouts is that switch?

Client: *It's on the inside. In my gut. I want to push it, but it's so small. I can't.*

Facilitator: And inside, in your gut. And you want to push it, but it's so small., you can't. And when you can't, what needs to happen to make it color mode?

Client: *I need some help. I need someone to push it for me.*

Facilitator: And what kind of someone is a someone who could push it for you?

Client: *Someone with smaller fingers.*

Facilitator: And can someone with smaller fingers push it for you?

Client: *Yes, yes! It's down now.*

5. **Maturing a Changed Landscape:** When a change occurs, your client (1) learns more about the change, (2) revisits the previously existing metaphor landscape to see what else may have shifted, and (3) moves forward in time as their landscape evolves.

Example continued:

Facilitator:	And switch is down now. And when switch is down, what happens to black and white mode?
Client:	It's switched off. Now I'm in color mode.
Facilitator:	And now you're in color mode. And when you're in color mode, what happens next?
Client:	Now the grass is green again, and it's not so long. I can walk on it. And there are red and blue flowers.
Facilitator:	And red and blue flowers, and the grass is green again and not so long. And you can walk on it. And is there anything else about that walk on it?
Client:	I don't feel so tired anymore. This is great!
Facilitator:	And when green grass and red and blue flowers, and you can walk on the path, what happens to feel more joy in your life?
Client:	Oh, that's all changed now. Now, I can walk down *the path. I can dance or run or skip down the path if I want to. And it's okay to be excited.*

Naturally, there are more things along the way that you could have explored in this session. Who, for example, was it that pushed on the button? Surely a resource! Or you may have noticed the client's last comment: "*It's okay to be excited*," hinting some sort of permission has been given. That may warrant exploring as well; you could go back to identifying a new metaphor for *excited* and develop more information about it. Or you might ask, "And where could that *okay* come from?"

All roads lead to more information about your client's inner world. Which roads you select depends upon the time you have available, your client's goals, the type of helping or healing you offer professionally, the sort of information you are there to help your client discover, and of course, where your client leads.

One Step Back and Two Steps Forward

With that tantalizing overview of the whole Symbolic Modeling process in mind, let's review the basics covered in *Basics Part One*. You will have opportunities to practice David Grove's Clean Language Questions that you have learned so far and Lawley and Tompkins' REPROCess model. As we review, I will add some additional food for thought.

Metaphors Revisited

You may remember from *Basics Part One* that metaphors can be divided into four categories:

Overt Metaphors: An obvious comparison of two unlike things that share some quality(ies). Ex.: "Life is a box of chocolates."

Embedded Metaphors: An often *overlooked* comparison of a thing or experience to something that is similar in some significant manner. This use of words is so *integral* to how we talk and think that we are often unaware of the implied metaphor. Ex.: "Chess *challenges* me to *focus* on strategy." (Note: All of these italicized words could imply metaphors.)

Embodied Metaphors: Since we perceive the world through our senses, we naturally tend to use our sensory experiences when encoding those experiences in metaphors. Ex.: "I've got *butterflies in my stomach* just thinking about it." "It *warms* my heart." "My troubles are *behind* me now." "I'll *weigh* my options." "The displeasure in his expression was *deafening*."

Gestural Metaphors: When a client uses their body to suggest an object or a space, perhaps with implied characteristics. Ex. "Hold it right there," with hand held up, palm side out, suggesting a stop sign.

Why Use Metaphors?

I am confident that, if you experienced your own metaphors as a client in *Basics Part One*, you are a believer that personal metaphors matter. Even if you can't quite put into words what happens when you delve into your metaphor landscape, you can tell it is profoundly and powerfully different than considering yourself from a cognitive perspective. If you have used Clean Language and Symbolic Modeling to work with clients, I am sure your clients have made some remarkable discoveries and perhaps experienced significant changes. We explored a number of reasons to use client-generated metaphors in the *Basics Part One* workbook. Here are several more to consider.

Client Awareness

Using your client's own metaphors means you are accessing information and beliefs that are often below their conscious awareness, for they come from their much larger subconscious world. When a particular problem or desired outcome is explored using CL and SyM, the metaphors that emerge reflect what is relevant to your client's system and needs, rather than what you or even your client may *assume* is relevant.

We can describe a Symbolic Modeling session as a process whereby metaphors emerge from the subconscious into conscious awareness, are *reprocessed*, and then reintegrated back into the subconscious. A client may consciously recall metaphors from their session for many years, calling on resourceful ones in times of need. They may consciously forget other metaphors in minutes. Either way, the metaphors are filed away in their subconscious, once again covertly guiding them.

Multicultural and Multi-generational Clients

Because you are working *cleanly* from your client's world-view, Clean Language is especially useful when you have a client whose background, culture, and/or generation differs from yours. When you, as the facilitator, are guided by your client's desired outcomes and metaphors, you significantly reduce the influence of your biases and assumptions and the possibility of misunderstanding or disconnecting from your client. You can be assured you are working within your client's value system and cultural expectations.

Integrating with Other Approaches

Attuning to your client's metaphors and staying *clean* can be of enormous help to you regardless of what therapeutic process or helping modality you use. Clean Language and Symbolic Modeling offer flexible tools that can enhance many other ways of working. (For further discussion, see page 144.)

1.1 *Activity*

The more you practice, the better you will get at hearing your clients' metaphors. Underline the metaphors in the following statements.

1. I realize now that my expectations were sky high. It's little wonder I was getting nowhere. Time to get my feet back on the ground and learn to live within my budget constraints. I'm sure I can find a house I'll like if I let go of that ideal image I've been fixated on!

2. Getting myself motivated to actually start a new project is always the hardest part for me. Once I'm out of the starting gate, the momentum carries me. And each item accomplished just spurs me on to add still another.

3. It seemed like a good idea at the time, but now I'm waffling. We've got a great committee assembled, but they're all so strong-willed! It may be that we have too many commanders and not enough sailors to just man the oars. How do we get out of this one?

4. I've come to a fork in the road. Deciding which way to go is tearing me apart! Ask me which way I want to go. One day, I'm sure I should major in engineering. But the next day, I'm equally sure I should study economics, though just what I'd do with that degree is not so clear.

5. I'm overwhelmed by the clutter in my office! Every pile demands my attention, and I'm stressed that something important has gotten buried somewhere, and I'm going to miss an important deadline.

Answers in the back.

Need more practice? Take newspaper or magazine articles: they are full of metaphors. In particular, look for the embedded ones, as they often *whiz by faster* than you can *catch* them in normal conversation (like you will need to do with your clients). Practice by underlining them. Listen for metaphor use among colleagues, friends, and family. And, naturally, notice your own!

If you are working with clients, a great way to practice is to tape a session (with permission, of course) and transcribe it or use one of the free transcription services you can find online. Then, at your leisure, you can study it for the metaphors you may have missed the first time around. This may prove to be particularly interesting, as you may find metaphors hinted at early in the session that you and your client did not recognize until later, when they become more overt. There are lots of other ways to use transcripts to learn, some of which we will get to in Section Six.

Reviewing Your CLQs

Look over this next chart that lists the Clean Language Questions you learned in *Basics Part One* as they might logically flow in a session. If it has been awhile since you have used them, read them aloud slowly and rhythmically. Decide if you need to go back to Part One to review anything. When you are ready, you can use the chart to practice devising questions for Activity 1.2. You might want to make a copy of this chart (and any others you find useful) to sit beside your workbook to refer to when doing Activities.

CHART: Sample Symbolic Modeling Session Progression

SAMPLE SESSION PROGRESSION

Desired Outcome: And what would you like to have happen?

Client:	*I want to feel more joy in my life.*
Acknowledge:	**And** *you want to feel more joy in your life.*
Focus attention:	**And when** *more joy in your life,*

Metaphor: That's *joy* **like what?**

Client:	*It's like dancing to a beautiful song instead of being a wallflower.*
Acknowledge:	**And it's like** *dancing to a beautiful song.*
Focus attention:	**And when** *dancing to a song,*

Attributes:	**Is there anything else about** *dancing?* **What kind of** *song* **is that** *song?*
Location:	**And whereabouts is** *dancing?*
Time:	**What happens just before** *dancing?* **Then what happens?**
Source:	**Whereabouts could that** *song* **come from?**
Relationship:	**And when** *dancing*, **is there anything else about** *song?* **And when** *dancing* **and** *beautiful song*, **is there a relationship between that** *dancing* **and that** *beautiful song?*

1.2 *Activity*

Practice repeating these clients' exact words and ask three **different** CLQs.

1. I just sense I can trust that light, that source of energy.

2. I want to be the kind of leader who nurtures the potential talents of my employees.

3. I want to plant a seed where the soil is rich and nourishing.

4. I feel a spring of creativity here, in my abdomen, ready to well up.

5. A large lion greets me at the portal, and I feel his sacred power is for me.

6. I'm holding an old-fashioned spyglass, and I'm looking out over a verdant valley with lots of individual farms.

7. We're floating on a raft on a vast sea, and a pod of dolphins is circling around us.

8. I want to be the kind of risk-taker who knows the difference between reaching for the gold and being foolhardy.

9. I want to feel rooted in my True Self, assured and steady.

10. When I sit for my qualifying exams, I want my attention to settle into focus.

More About Metaphors

Enacting metaphors

A way of working with your client's metaphors that may be new to you is to have them physically get up and move through their landscape. As they step into the space a symbol occupies, they perceive from that symbol's perspective; they may experience its emotion; they tap into its wisdom. And as they take on information from that symbol, they may make all sorts of new discoveries.

You may find this useful for a client who:

- Jumps from one metaphor to another to another that they perceive as examples of the same thing, not staying with any single metaphor long enough to develop it
- Is dominantly kinesthetic and likes this way of exploring their landscape
- Is getting sleepy, dissociating, or otherwise having difficulty focusing
- Enjoys working in a variety of ways
- Is having difficulty discovering some information, such as a symbol's intentions.

Examples:

A client wants to *"push back against an encroaching wall."* You can invite them to stand up and demonstrate that *push back*. Then you might ask, "And is there anything else about that push back?"

A client says they are *"going around and around in circles."* You can invite them to get up and go *around and around in circles.* You might ask, "And as you're going around and around, what happens next?"

A client declares they are *"painted into a corner."* You can invite them to find a corner that is like the one they are *painted into*. You might ask, "And what would you like to have happen when painted into a corner… like that?"

Remember to stay *clean*! Resist the urge to choose the encroaching wall, suggest how big the circles may be by gesturing, or subtly decide how confined a space your client's corner is by where you place yourself.

A welcome advantage of enacting metaphors is that, with the symbols the client describes right in front of you, most facilitators are able to stay clean and accurate without having to take as many notes. You also don't need to do lengthy repeating because the presence of the elements will keep them psychoactive for the client, though you'll no doubt do some repeating to direct attention to specifics. Less work for you will mean you have more mental bandwidth to be closely listening to and tracking your client.

Steps for Enacting Metaphors

1. First, help your client verbally develop attributes about their landscape's multiple symbols and clearly identify their locations. You could also have your client make a metaphor map.

2. Establish a space in the room or outdoors, and invite your client to use the space as if it were their metaphor landscape. The first time with a client, you may need to explain this conversationally (i.e., not using CLQs, though you should remain *clean*). Have them locate key symbols in the space, marking them in any way they wish. Thereafter, you can make the invitation to explore the various spaces sound more like a CL directive: "*And go to [symbol].*" If the symbol was originally in an internal location, you can suggest your client, "*Find a space that knows about that [x], there* (as you gesture towards its location in the client's body)." You can use this same directive to have your client find an alternative space if their first choice for a location is out of reach or in a potentially dangerous spot, like in a tree or on a shaky chair or tabletop.

3. Continue exploring symbols and their relationships with other symbols by moving your client to their locations using your regular Clean Language Questions. Recall your activity in *Basics Part One* (Section Four): Clean Space and Enough/More than Enough/Not Enough. You can move your client around similarly, saying, "*Go to [x location].*" and then ask, "*And what do you know from there?*" or "*And when [x], is there anything else about that [x]?*" or any other CLQ you choose.

Physicalizing metaphors

You are most familiar with this approach when having your client draw a metaphor map to begin or end a session. Physicalizing metaphors refers to putting the symbol into some kind of physical form. It might be by drawing or by working with clay or sand, for example. Or you can have your client put words for symbols on Post-It notes and place them about the space, experiencing the whole. Be creative with what materials you have on hand and encourage your client to be creative using them! The more generic and open-ended they are, the *cleaner* they will be.

You may find this useful in many of the same situations listed above for enacting metaphors. It is also helpful to:

- Aid your client in holding a large amount of information in mind at one time

- Save your client's information over a period of time or sessions so that they can acknowledge change and growth, notice patterns, and/or notice what is not there

- Consider what is beyond their presently known landscape

At the end of a session, I will often encourage a client to take a picture with their cell phone of their Post-its or whatever else they've used as a way to recall their experience.

1.3 *Activity*

Partner practice: Take turns facilitating one another as clients *enact* their metaphor landscape. Begin by having each of you create a **Before our Session** sheet. The Facilitator invites the Client to describe their drawing, asking a few CLQs to gather some information about the metaphors and encourage the client to enter their symbolic domain. Once the Client is pyschoactively engaged, Facilitator invites the Client to use the space around them to lay out the metaphor landscape.

Before Our Session...

To begin our session, consider this question. Feel free to write as little or as much as you like.

What would you like to have happen?

In the space below or on another sheet of paper, do a drawing of what this issue is like for you now and a second drawing of what you would like it to be like. NO artistic talent is required here; stick figures are fine.

Concept by Penny Tompkins and James Lawley

Once some metaphors are located and marked by something in the area or on Post-its, the Facilitator develops the landscape with CLQs. You may want to use the chart on page 8 or page 21. You may also want to use the specialized question below that works beautifully when working with spatial processes. Once the client settles in on or near a new space, and looks up for a question, ask:

"And what do you know from there?"

Now that you have had an opportunity to review some of what you learned in *Basics Part One*, what I will give you in the remainder of this Section and the next are some refining tips about the ways you ask and the way you can use your Clean questions. Perhaps you have wondered about some of these details as you practiced with clients.

Words within Words

It is considered perfectly *clean* to separate multi-syllabic or compound words into their parts and ask a CLQ about one or more parts. Often, we no longer notice a word embedded within a word, but the subconscious notices what we consciously may not. A client never picks a word entirely randomly. Even if there is no obvious logical connection, you can point out the embedded word with your question and see what happens. The associations your client makes can lead to surprising discoveries.

But don't get carried away with this! Your client's words are not fodder for word games to entertain you. If you have tried this once or twice, and your client does not find it helpful, I suggest you cease and desist. You don't want to break rapport by having your client feel like you are playing and not "getting" them. But once in a blue moon, you may get an intuitive hit to ask about a word's parts.

Listen, too, for words that sound similar or the same. Words that can be spelled differently may suggest more than one meaning. Both may be relevant in the client's landscape. Clients can get remarkably creative without consciously intending to be! I have had a number of fascinating things happen for clients with the word *know*, for example. Clients discovered relationships between *no* and *know*, *gnome* and *know*, and a *nose* that *knows*. In each instance, the client located a place of deep intuitive knowing after first finding the similar sounding word or object.

Example:

Client: *I'm on a highway, driving at breakneck speed.*

Facilitator: And a highway and driving at breakneck speed. And when *break*neck, is there anything else about that break?

Client: *Yes. Yes, it's something about breaking... breaking away from, breaking off with. I want to break away from someone who's driving behind me, but I'm scared to go too fast. And I'm worried, if I put on the brakes, I'll skid out of control!*

More About Clean Language Syntax

Specifying *that* [x]

With each new Clean Language Question you learned, I trust you have been carefully using its exact wording. We considered in *Basics Part One* why you start every sentence with *And*. Let's consider now why you use the word *that* in front of the client's word(s).

Example:

Client: *I've always sought my father's respect.*

Facilitator: And always sought your father's respect. And when father's respect, what kind of respect is *that* respect?

You are narrowing your client's attention to *that* respect *specifically*. I have used an example where it probably seems obvious to refer to that specifically, for one's father's respect very likely has a unique role in anyone's life. *But the same could be true for any symbol.*

Example:

Client: *I can almost reach the gold ring.*

Facilitator: And can almost reach the gold ring. And when gold ring, what kind of gold ring is that gold ring?

By using the word *that*, you encourage your client to zoom in on their particular symbol for more details. Were you to ask, "And is there anything else about a gold ring?", your wording could encourage your client to go cognitive, to think about gold rings in general or even other particular gold rings. Of course, your client could do that in answer to your question even if you include *that*. But there is a ***specificity*** and a ***rhythm*** to using the word *that* that works well.

Using *I* or *You*

You may have been wondering, if your client refers to themselves as *I*, is it *clean* to change the *I* to *you*? Either is considered *clean*. Personally, as you may have noticed, I always change the pronoun to you. As a client, I find I am very distracted by my facilitator using my personal pronoun. Inside, I am thinking, "No, not you. Me!" I stop my facilitator, and request that they change it. Most trainees I have worked with feel the same way, though others have not cared one way or the other. I have never had a client stop me and request that I use *I*. But the choice is yours.

There is one exception I make, and that is if the client is describing some positive self-talk, something they say to themselves that is motivating, encouraging, or acknowledging in some helpful way. I want to echo such phrases.

Example:

Client: *I did it! I did it! I just kept saying to myself, "I can make it! Don't give up." And I didn't.*

Facilitator: And you did it! And "I can make it!" And "Don't give up!" And when "I can make it!", what happens just before you say to yourself, "I can make it!"?

Client: *I feel a glow of determination in my solar plexus. But it is steely, too, like molten steel. When I felt that, I knew I could do it.*

Notice I said I do this if the self-talk is encouraging. I wouldn't say, "And disheartened. And "I'm worthless!". Why reinforce that kind of self-talk?!

Using *Here* or *There*

You can apply the same logic to using *here* or *there* as you do to using *I* or *you.*

Example:

Client: *(Laying a hand on her chest) Calm is here, in my heart.*

Facilitator: (Gesturing [not pointing!] towards client's chest) And calm, there, in your heart. And when calm, whereabouts there,... in your heart,... is calm?

You can, of course, repeat *here* exactly, but using *there* is considered *clean* as well.

Using *When* or *As*

You have been beginning the middle phrase of the full three part Clean Language syntax with the word *when.* In so doing, you invite your client to narrow their attention to a particular segment of time and conditions and a particular set of words or images about which you plan to ask a Clean Language Question.

Example:

Client: *There is some sort of scuffle outside, and now two men are knocking at the door.*

Facilitator: And scuffle outside, and two men, knocking at the door. And **when** men knocking, what kind of knocking is that knocking?

Now, you can continue to use *when* to frame the experience your specific question addresses and it will work fine, but consider the subtle difference of substituting *as* for *when.* It is a useful variation to use when your client is engaged in imagining some action *in the moment.* It invites attention to the *experience* as it unfolds, rather than your client's observation of it.

Example:

Client: *I've waited so long for this. And now I take the stage. I earned it, and I'm ready.*

Facilitator: And you're ready. And you earned it. And you take the stage. And **as** you take the stage, then what happens?

Client: *I'm thinking that I'm proud of myself!*

Variations in Repetition

More Repetition

Up to this point, we have been using the three-part, full syntax model of Clean Language questions, but I would like to introduce you to another, very rhythmical variation you might use. Like the use of the word *that*, it encourages the client to concentrate on their particular, specific statement.

If you have heard me facilitate a client, you may have noticed I often add repetitions of my client's words *after* the Clean Language Question.

Example:

Client: *I'm in a tunnel, and I'm frightened, but I'm determined to get out.*

Facilitator: And you're in a tunnel and frightened…and you're determined to get out. And when determined to get out, that's determined… like what,… when you're in a tunnel,… and you're determined to get out?

Let's examine my choices. With my first repetition, "*And you're in a tunnel and frightened,*" I am acknowledging my client's embodied experience, what they are sensing. They says they are frightened, so they made it pretty clear this is a problem. They have already implied their desired outcome: to get out, so I don't need to ask for that. My question is intended to help them notice their resource state, their determination, which could help them achieve their desired outcome.

It may be fear that is motivating my client's determination to get out, in which case it would be a resource…but it just doesn't feel necessary for me to test this possibility right now. Notice my reliance on my intuitive sense to make choices; you simply can't explore every possibility. But you *can* be alert to hints that something you passed over is, in fact, relevant. I won't dismiss the possibility that my client's fear could prove helpful to them.

I choose to start by asking for a metaphor for *determined*. And then I emphasize their motivated state by repeating their descriptive words *again*. I find it particularly helpful to use this added repetition of a key phrase after the question when:

1. You are looking to enhance the client's embodied experience of a resourceful *feeling* or *sensation*.

2. The client is considering several thoughts or multiple symbols at once. With a lot of information to consider, it helps to repeat key words again after your question.

3. The repetition imbues your question with a *rhythmic, trance-inducing quality* that is not like ordinary conversation. This helps your client stay in a mindful, inner-focused state.

Less Repetition

Just as there are good reasons to add additional repetitions of words or phrases at times, there are good reasons at other times for deliberately choosing *not* to use a CLQ's three-part, full syntax.

Example:

Client: *I'm determined to get out. I'm just forcing my way through the ditch, through the water.*

Facilitator: And determined and forcing your way. And then what happens?

Here the client has momentum; they are on the move in the direction of the change they want. This is a situation in which you might choose not to slow them down. You keep up with their forceful pace by keeping your sentences short and moving them ahead with a future time question.

When shortening the full CL syntax, depending on your strategy and intent, you can leave out:

The first acknowledgment phrase
or
The second "And when" phrase
or
Both, asking only the question

When to Use Fewer or More Repetitions

- Do you want to slow down your client to notice something, get additional information, or stay with a feeling? Then use more repetitions, not fewer.

- Perhaps your client is doing a great job of self-modeling, discovering and examining a lot on their own, keeping the landscape very much alive, and you want to keep your presence as minimal as possible. You might just ask a few CLQs with no repetitions.

Choose your repetitions mindfully. You will no doubt develop your own style of placing repetitions, your own rhythm, your own reasoning as to when to use full syntax and when to curtail it.

Be curious about the effects different orders and different amounts of repetition have on your clients. Experiment with variations!

Having your own personal experiences as a client with several facilitators will greatly inform your own facilitating. You will undoubtedly viscerally experience the differences individual styles of voice, pacing, and repetitions make.

To Repeat or Not to Repeat?

Some clients (and I happen to be one of them) have a pattern of saying both what something *is* and what it *is not*. Sometimes I am feeling my way to an accurate description. Sometimes it just seems like a more complete explanation. Or... who knows why this pattern persists? Whatever the reason, as the facilitator, most of the time I recommend you not repeat what the something is *not*. It is like saying, "Don't think of the elephant in the room." You have to think of an elephant first, and then negate that thought. But you want your client's whole focus on what is true for them. If your client has said, "It's [x], not [y]," just repeat the [x] part.

Example:

Client: *Its shell is not solid, exactly; it's actually porous. That way it's flexible, not rigid.*

Facilitator: And porous shell and flexible. And when porous, is there anything else about that porous?

I make an exception for times when my client has been struggling with a problem for some time, usually with a lot of emotion involved. When a shift finally occurs, I have the sense that when my client says what [x] is not *any longer*, it is soothing self-talk. That I will repeat, though I will not ask more CLQs about it, because it is no longer their reality.

Example:

Client: *I've been afraid for so long, but now, with my angel at my side, I'm not afraid anymore. I feel safe.*

Facilitator: And your angel at your side. And not afraid anymore. And you feel safe. And when you feel safe, whereabouts is that feel safe?

1.4 Activity

Here are some longer client statements. Practice asking CLQs, taking all the time you need to decide what you will include in your repetitions. Practice at least two ways of saying each question, incorporating *more* or *less information* and *more* or *fewer repetitions*.

Example:

Client: *I'm the conductor of the orchestra. All the musicians are looking at me, waiting for my command. Everyone has tuned his or her instrument. Boy, am I sweating! But, you know, that's part of the fun: the tension, the anticipation.*

Facilitator: #1 And you're the conductor. And musicians looking. And tuned. And part of the fun, tension, anticipation! And when tension, what kind of tension is that tension, when it's part of the fun?

#2 And conductor of the orchestra. And all the musicians are looking at you. Waiting for your command. And fun, tension, anticipation. And when anticipation, is there anything else about that anticipation?

1. I want a relationship that's like having a dance partner. To be that close to someone, to feel connected and responsive. That would be heavenly!

2. It's like I'm at a buffet, and there is all this wonderful-looking food! I have a tray that fits just the right amount of food, and I am able to balance it without even thinking about it. It just happens naturally.

3. I'm looking for some kind of change, not just an ordinary change, a revolution. Things would really be different, and I would feel it.

4. I'm lying on a blanket, and a group of people are tossing me in the air, effortlessly. Everyone is smiling and laughing and having a good time. I'm having a good time, too, and I'm as light as air.

5. I sense an Old Soul nearby, standing close to me. She sees the real me. When I need her, she is there with the wisdom I need.

6. There is a system of gears and pulleys in my torso. Pull on one rope, and the whole system goes into motion. I know how to take care of it; the gears needs regular oiling to keep functioning.

7. I'm floating down a river, and there's a tree with light bark close to the bank. There aren't many of this type of tree, and I keep paying attention to this type. It's getting closer and closer.

8. I sense a column of energy, of light, that comes from above. It enters my crown chakra, and then goes down, down, down. It ends, still inside me, in a sacred space, a special place.

9. If I focus on my breathing, then I can center and stay calm. It is as if I can then bring everything to a single point of stillness, as long as I concentrate. In, out, down, down. Ah... yes.

10. I am the pilot of this airplane, and I am the flight attendant. I have to be taking care of all the passengers, and I have to guide the plane. Most of the time, it is on autopilot, but not all the time. The safety and well-being of all the passengers is my responsibility.

1.5 *Activity*

Time for a client or partner practice. Try going 25 minutes for each facilitator. You have a lot of questions and facilitating strategies to work with now. If it would help you, refer to the following chart, the one on page 8, or use one of your own creation.

Afterwards, answer the following questions:

Something I did well was:

Something I want to work on next time is:

CHART: 9 Basic Clean Language Questions

9 Basic Clean Language Questions
where [x] stands for a client's words or non-verbals

P/R/O

And what would you like to have happen?

And then what happens?

DEVELOPING CLQs

And that's [x]...like what?

And is there anything else about that?

And what kind of [x] is that [x]?

And where/whereabouts is that [x]?

And what happens just before [x]?

And then what happens?/And what happens next?

And where could that [x] come from?

And when [x] and when [y], is there a relationship between [x] and [y]?

More About Time

Peeling Apart "Sometimes"

When a client describes a "sometimes I [do x], sometimes I [do y]" situation, or similarly, "sometimes I [do x] and sometimes I don't [do x]," you could ask some variation of these questions:

> **"And when sometimes you** [do x]**, what kind of times are those times when you** [do x]**?"**
>
> **"And when sometimes you** [do y]**, is there anything else about those times when you** [do y]**?**

Example:

Client: *Sometimes, I wish the world would just go away, and sometimes I'm ready to take on whatever comes!*

Facilitator: And sometimes you wish the world would just go away. And sometimes you're ready to take on whatever comes! And when sometimes you're ready to take on whatever comes, what kind of times are those times?

Client: *They're when I'm rested.*

Facilitator: And rested. And is there anything else about those times when you're ready to take on whatever comes?

Keep on asking, "And is there anything else about those times?" for as long as your client is discovering new things about any state they have identified as resourceful. You can also explore the times when your client's not in a resourceful state to learn more about how that happens, especially if it keeps happening again and again, suggesting a pattern. Problems can get clarified so your client can get a desired outcome for them. *But don't keep your client's attention on un-resourceful feelings for very long; you will only reinforce that experience.* Remember: In REPROCess, we want to model the client's resources and desired outcomes.

Moving Forward in Time

It is tempting to keep your client moving forward in time, to repeatedly ask, "And then what happens?" There is a general tendency among helping professionals to want to facilitate a client to "progress," to press towards solutions and action steps. Slow down! Take your time developing all parts of the landscape. As long as new information is emerging from your CLQs, your client is gathering more to meet whatever is coming. Perhaps resources will be strengthened or new ones revealed. Perhaps new problems will emerge that need to be addressed, for they could undermine later efforts to change. It is not your job to push your client towards taking any action, to force any change; your job is to help them learn about their system, their landscape and to get ready for whatever they decide they want to do, whenever that is. You cannot force transformational change even if you try, any more than your client can. It happens when it happens, when all is ready. Resist the urge to push your client along with the intention of getting the problem fixed.

Mind the Gap

You have learned the CLQs that direct your client's attention forward and backwards in time. You may be surprised by how precisely you can splice time. Be curious about what happens in small gaps, such as those between two actions or between a thought and an action, for example. You can ask:

> **"And what happens after** [x] **and before** [y]**?"**

Example:

Client: *He walked in the room, and I had to leave immediately.*

Facilitator: And he walked in. And you had to leave. And when walked in and leave immediately, what happened *after* he walked in and *before* you had to leave immediately?

Client: *I remembered my father, and I just felt overwhelmed.*

How easily might you have assumed this client's reaction was all about the man who walked in? Exploring time gaps is likely to bring out more information and can reveal significant blocks and crucial choice points. Many a mystifying situation can be untangled and pivotal issue unearthed when keen attention is paid to what is happening in the gaps!

1.6 Activity

With these client statements, practice exploring what might be happening between occurrences, which could be thoughts, feelings, or actions. Write out and say aloud what you would ask.

CLQ: "And what happens after [x] and before [y]?"

1. I see a little girl playing with her dog in the park, and I just have to smile.

2. I came in this morning determined to talk to my boss about the way my supervisor harasses me, but I chickened out.

3. I can feel the butterflies in my stomach, but I don't let them stop me.

4. First, I am in the audience, watching the stage, and then somehow I am the one who is on the stage, facing the audience.

5. I come to a brick wall with an old door in it, the kind that is really heavy and rounded at the top. I'm not sure I should open it, but then I do.

Developing a Sequence

You may notice in the examples above that a *sequence* of occurrences has begun to emerge. I use the broad term occurrences, as it may include internal thoughts, feelings, actions, and reactions by the client and by their metaphors, as well as events and happenings.

As the facilitator, you are assisting your client in deconstructing their internal logic and the sequencing of occurrences in their patterns. We will be delving into this much more deeply when we get into change work. For now, concentrate on being on the lookout for clues about time and sequence information in your client's landscape.

Here are commonly used words that suggest a sequence. Attuning to these can help you increase your awareness of when a client is describing a pattern--unwanted or wanted. It may only just be emerging, and your Clean questions can help it come fully to light. Consider these words/phrases:

until	before	while	as
if...then	after	because...then	anytime
when...then	therefore	first...then/next/second	wherever
always	often	sometimes	whenever

1.7 *Activity*

List other words or phrases that could potentially suggest a sequence.

Section One Summary

Metaphors reveal your client's subconscious world or system, quickly uncovering information and beliefs to which your client may have no conscious access.

You can effectively serve **multicultural** and **multi-generational populations** using metaphors and Clean Language because they limit the influence of your biases and assumptions.

Enacting and **physicalizing** metaphors are creative methods you can use to enhance your client's experiential exploration.

Repetition: By varying which words, how often, and where in your phrasing you repeat client's words, you can manipulate different rhythms, emphases, and experiential effects.

Your job is not to be a **problem-solver**. Resist the urge to push your client with the intention of getting the problem fixed.

Exploring small gaps in the time between two occurrences (thoughts, feelings, actions, events) can reveal important information about your client'smetaphor landscape and process.

My take-away from this section is...

Questions I have...

Invitation: If you want to learn more about Enacting and Physicalizing Metaphors by working with drawings or with space, you will find lots of information and ideas in my book, *Panning for Your Client's Gold: 12 Lean Clean Language Processes* (Find in Resources)

1.8 *Review Activity*

Practice asking at least three CLQs of each example. Vary your repetition choices. Use the chart on page 8 to help.

1. It's as if I have planted a new seed, and it's ready to grow and grow.

2. I have a fountain in my gut, and when it's flowing, I'm filled with a really healing sense of loving and potential and wholeness.

3. Where I come from, multiple generations of families live together, and I sense the continuity of support and interdependence at the same time.

4. I have this underlying feeling that everything's going to come out all right; I just have to be more patient.

5. I'm walking in what looks like a zoo of some kind, and I'm passing cages, but the animals inside them are not what you think of as zoo animals. They're like house cats and poodles. And now it's clear to me: I'm here to set them free, me, the one with opposable thumbs!

Section Two

"Problems are not the problem;
coping is the problem."

-Virginia Satir

You will recall the handy acronym we use to describe Symbolic Modeling's strategy: REPROCess. We concentrated on the R-E-P-R-O categories in *Basics Part One*. It is not that we ignored the C for *change* entirely; greater clarity is, itself, a change. The clarity that comes from gathering information can foster further changes in thoughts, feelings, and actions. We will get on to working with more involved change work and specific questions and strategies designed to support it in Sections Four and Five. But first, let's add some new considerations to the REPRO- portion of the model as we revisit our 9 CLQs and SyM strategies.

Reviewing REPROCess

REPROCess: An acronym for the model developed by James Lawley and Penny Tompkins. I think of it as a way to categorize the *kind of information* I am hearing as my client speaks. Different kinds of information suggest where to direct my client's attention-- either towards or away from. For example, if it is a Resource, I will ask developing questions to elicit its attributes. If it a Problem, I will ask, "And what would you like to have happen?" to get a desired outcome, and so on.

(R) Resources (E) Explanations (P) Problem (R) Remedy (O) Desired Outcome (C) Change and -ess for its part in *reprocessing*.

Take note here. When I say this model helps you determine what information you ask Clean Language Questions about, I do not mean you go into a Symbolic Modeling session with predetermined intentions for what your client should do. REPROCess helps you develop a strategy for *responding* to your client's landscape. It is not intended to dictate outcomes for your client or to push change.

REPROCess is not the only guiding strategy you can use with Clean Language; David Grove developed multiple processes that employed different strategies for how to help people heal, grow, and change. But it is what we work with in these *Basics* workbooks as the fundamental navigational tool of the Symbolic Modeling, as developed by James Lawley and Penny Tompkins.

More About Resources

Resources are those things that have value to your client because they identify them as helpful to them in some way. Getting to know a resource or resource state better may be all it takes for your client's desired outcome to be realized, as they embrace and/or strengthen a capacity they didn't know they had. You gather information, or what we call *develop* a resource, with Clean Language Questions so your client can:

- **discover** what it can do for them
- **locate** it so they can find it again when they need it
- **learn how to utilize** it effectively

Example:

Client:	*I'd like to feel more confident*	*(Desired Outcome Statement #1)*
Facilitator:	And you'd like to feel more confident. And when feel more confident, what kind of confident is that confident?	(Develop attributes)
Client:	*It's a strong confident.*	*(Awareness of an attribute)*
Facilitator:	And a strong confident. And when you feel a strong confident, where do you feel that confident?	(Location CLQ #1)
Client:	*In my back.*	*(Awareness of location)*
Facilitator:	And in your back. And when in your back, where in your back?	(Location CLQ #2)
Client:	*Right along my spine.*	*(Awareness of location)*
Facilitator:	And right along your spine. And where right along your spine?	(Location CLQ #3)
Client:	*Around and inside my vertebrae.* *My whole spine.*	*(Awareness of location)*
Facilitator:	And around and inside...your whole spine. And is there anything else about that strong Confident, around and inside your vertebrae?	(Develop attributes)
Client:	*It's long and rigid.*	*(Awareness of attributes)*
Facilitator:	And long and rigid. And that's long and rigid...like what?	(Identify the metaphor)
Client:	*Like a tree, like a tall, straight tree.*	*(Awareness of attributes)*
Facilitator:	And a tall, straight tree. And when a tall, straight tree, whereabouts is that tree?	(Location CLQ #4: Verify location of the new metaphor)
Client:	*Right up my spine, on the inside.*	*(Awareness of location)*
Facilitator:	And up your spine, on the inside. And is there anything else about that tree, tall and straight, on the inside?	(Develop attributes)
Client:	*It's too flexible...and too thin.*	*(New problems)*

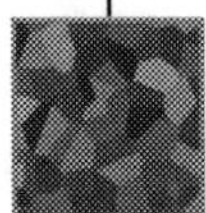

Facilitator:	And it's too flexible...too thin. And when too flexible and too thin, what would you like to have happen?	(Respond to a problem statement)
Client:	*I want it to be stronger.*	*(Desired Outcome Statement #2)*
Facilitator:	And when a tall tree...and too flexible...and too thin, and you want it to be stronger... and when you want to feel more confident, is there a relationship between a stronger tree... and feel more confident, a strong confident?	(Checking D.O. #1 with D.O. #2)
Client:	*Yes, they're the same.*	*(Embodied sense of own D.O.)*

Sometimes the information a client gets about the metaphor will be all they need; simply discovering the tree in their spine will help them access the feeling of confidence they want. But other times, as in the example above, the client discovers a problem(s) with the metaphor (i.e. the tree is too flexible and too thin). We will be addressing how to aid a client with this in Section Four when we get to Stage 4 of the SyM process: Getting Ready for Change. For now, let's consider resources in greater depth.

Resources Revealed

Lawley and Tompkins divide resources into three categories:

1. **Overt Resource:** The client identifies the symbol as a resource (whether or not it is clear how it will work).

   Examples:

   A wonderful set of gears in his head.
   A wise woman with a map in her hand.

2. **Latent Resource:** Its use is not obvious to the client. The resource may appear long before its help is required.

   Examples:

   A bucolic scene includes a pretty river. Much later, the client discovers they can use the water in the river to make the concrete needed to build themselves a solid foundation.

   The client notices a switch on the wall. Switches are meant to turn something on and off. What's this one for? Perhaps the client has no idea, at this time. Sometimes the switch is the first part to emerge in the landscape. But, as the client explores its attributes, or perhaps as other symbols emerge, they become aware of a generator that is needed to keep some crucial flow going. Only then is the resourceful nature of the switch revealed: it controls the generator!

3. **To-Be-Converted Resource**: Sometimes what appears to be unusable or even threatening may shift and become useful.

    Examples:

    The rope that binds his hands, once untied, is just what he needs to pull himself out of the well.

    The Gripper who clutches her shoulder, holding her back, becomes the Strong Man who keeps the Critical Eye's lid down.

Your client may clearly identify a desire to experience a resourceful feeling/state, to strengthen it, or get to know it better. Other times, they may hint at a resource but not have recognized its potential value. *Directing your* client's attention to noticing and developing emerging resources is one of your key functions as a facilitator.

Selecting Resources to Develop

In determining which resources to direct your client's attention towards, stick closely to the logic of your client's landscape, to *what they value*, and to *what they need* to enable them to accomplish their stated desired outcome.

This next client suggests that they have *self-control* and, as they want to exert it, presumably it is a valuable resource. I will help them learn more about their self-control. But I will also direct their attention to *exert*. With their choice of words, the client separates out the *exertion* of that control as a distinct issue. Notice, they don't say they want more or better self-control; they say they want to better *exert* the self-control they have.

Example:

Client: *I want to **exert** my self-control better.*

Facilitator: And you want to exert your self-control better. And when self-control, what kind of control is that control?

Client: *It's control of my temper, of what I say to others when I'm riled up. And control of when I say it.*

Facilitator: And control of your temper, of what you say when you're riled up and when you say it. And when self-control like that, what kind of self that self?

Client: *It's a patient self who knows how to bide her time. A self who can exert control over her impatience.*

Facilitator: And a self who can exert control. And when exert, what kind of exert is that exert?

Client: *(Clenching and unclenching her fists) It's a strong exert, almost instinctive.*

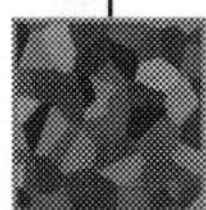

The client's gestures suggest a metaphor, though she may not have noticed it. Often, it takes just one question to bring it to conscious awareness.

Example continued:

Facilitator: And strong and instinctive...and (mirrors clenching and gestures towards client's hands). And when [clenching gesture], what kind of [gesture] is that [gesture]?

Client: *(Looking at her hands, laughs) Oh! They're reins. I'm holding the reins, holding myself back. Or trying to. I'm not being very successful at it.*

Facilitator: And reins. And you're holding the reins. And trying to hold yourself back. And when you're not being very successful at it, what would you like to have happen?

Client: *I want to get better at keeping a steady pressure on the reins. I get excited about the race, and I stop holding back. I want to get better at holding myself back, biding my time for the long run, letting others have their turn at the front of the pack, too.*

Look at all the facilitator might have missed helping to reveal had they not be listening so closely to the client who wanted to *exert* control! Or perhaps the resource metaphor would have emerged anyway with questions about control. We can't know; there's no way to rewind the session and see what would happen if different questions were asked. But sometimes, I can't help but feel that a keen question about something the client said, that they may have paid no attention to, is just what was needed.

2.1 *Activity*

In these sentences, first underline a **resource** that the client values. (Note: There may be more than one.) Use your CLQs to **develop information** about the words in the statement and get a **metaphor** for the resource. (You might want to reference the chart on page 21 or use one of your own.) Write out your questions and practice saying them out aloud at a slow, rhythmic pace. If you have a practice buddy, they can take on the role of the client.

1. When I get up in front of a class, I get this high energy focus that helps me be very present with my students.

2. Envisioning my success keeps me plugging away in spite of setbacks.

3. Meditation takes me to a quiet place, and that helps me stay balanced.

4. Our mission statement not only gives our team a clear sense of common purpose, it inspires us, too!

5. I'm sure my debating skills will help me stand out from the crowd of applicants.

More About Source

Interestingly, the **source of a resource**, whether the resource is a symbol or an attribute, is often more useful and/or powerful than the resource itself. It may have new information as well. To find the most resourceful resource, *you may need to ask the source question several times*.

"And where/whereabouts could that [x resource] come from?"

Example:

Client: *I'm looking down at my feet, and there are a pair of ruby slippers on them.*

Facilitator: And a pair of ruby slippers. And when ruby slippers, whereabouts could those slippers come from?

Client: *Glinda the Good Witch gave them to me. She knows they're powerful, but she doesn't know what kind of power they have.*

Facilitator: And they're powerful. And when power, where could that power come from?

Client: *Well, I don't know how I know this 'cause it's not like in the story, but there seems to be another witch. Not of the West or the East, not Glinda...it's a Witch Above All Witches.*

Facilitator: And a Witch Above All Witches. And where could a Witch Above All Witches come from?

Client: *She serves The One. The One decides who has what powers, who keeps them, who loses them, who earns them back. Yes, there's something about earning.*

This client has now found a new Witch and the One, both of whom might be more powerful than the ruby slippers. Are they all the available resources? Keep asking about the source of the resources until you reach the end of what is currently in your client's awareness. Then you and/or your client can decide which to explore further with CLQs. Trust your client's intuitive sense.

Example continued:

Facilitator: And where could The One come from?

Client: *The One doesn't come from anywhere. The One just is. It's always been there. It knows all and controls all. It's loving, even if the witches it gives power to are not.*

Facilitator: And when The One knows all, controls all, and is loving and when ruby slippers, is there a relationship between The One and ruby slippers?

Client: *Ah, yes! The One gives them their power. And it wants me to have them now.*

2.2 *Activity*

Write out questions that ask for the *source* of a *resource* in the following client statements. A practice buddy can take on the client role and create further answers to work with. This is also another opportunity to practice varying amounts of repetition.

1. I feel a sense of newfound calm. I can take a deep breath, and just do what I need to do.

2. I'm walking along the banks of a river, and I need to get to the other side. A movement catches my eye, and I notice some rope. It's a rope bridge connecting the two sides.

3. I realize that, in order to have a really productive session, I need to take some time to get centered and focused before I start writing.

4. I'm exhausted, and I find a little cabin. I enter. It's just one room, and there's a soft bed and a warm fire in the fireplace, like it's all been waiting for me.

5. I feel a Loving Presence just behind my right shoulder. I don't know who it is; I can tell it's a woman. She's always there behind me, sort of protecting me, but not taking over.

6. I'm in a deep well with stone sides. One side is slick and wet. The other is dry. There are rings embedded into the rocks where I can get a handhold and a foothold on this side.

More About P/R/O

As you have discovered by now, clients' statements do not always fall neatly into a linear sequence: 1) Problem, 2) Remedy, and 3) Outcome. Sometimes, clients lump them together in the same sentence, and you need to tease them apart. What do you ask if your client's statement includes more than one category? The answer is, it depends.

Remember, your ultimate goal is to have a clearly defined desired outcome(s). If your client gives a desired outcome and it seems directly related to the problem, then you might set aside the problem statement and go right to developing the desired outcome, as in this example.

Example:

Client: *I'm too tired in the mornings at work, and I want to get more rest.* (P., D.O.)

Facilitator: And too tired. And want to get more rest. And what kind of rest is that rest you want to get more of?

Another pairing of a problem and a desired outcome could suggest that more information about the problem(s) might be helpful to get a clearer picture of what the issue(s) are and how many desired outcomes are involved. Just be careful not to get lured into *developing* the problem!

Example:

Client: *What I really want to have is some time to think of the bigger picture, but I seem to spend most of my day putting out proverbial fires.* (D.O., P.)

Facilitator: And time to think of the bigger picture. And proverbial fires. And when proverbial fires, what kind of proverbial is that proverbial?

The client suggests time is an issue, and they have a problematic pattern that repeats. Maybe it is an issue of one person being responsible for too much. Maybe it is about trying to please too many people. Maybe it is about being too easily accessible to others. Maybe it is about not trusting others to take care of things. I certainly don't know, and perhaps my client isn't sure yet either. They could benefit from getting clearer about just what prevents them from having what they want. Focusing their attention solely on their first desired outcome may not be the most efficient use of your time together.

But don't worry. If you don't get to some key underlying issue(s) early in the session, Stages Four and Five of the Symbolic Modeling process, which we will cover in Sections Four and Five, help your client uncover them. Trust the process, and the truth will come out!

Tip: Did you wonder in the example above why I didn't ask about *fires*? It is because that might have invited lots of story-telling about specific examples that are not relevant to the client's inner experience. Instead I asked about *proverbial*, directing attention to the pattern-- to what might be consistent about all the fires. Something for you to ponder!

2.3 *Activity*

Are these Problem, Remedy or Desired Outcome statements? A combination of some sort? Identify P/R/Os, and write out your response using a variety of repetition choices (full syntax, fewer words, more words, in various order, etc.). Practice saying your statements/ questions *aloud*.

1. I want to explore this beach, but the sand is too hot!

2. I'm not interested in studying trigonometry, but I may have to take it because some colleges require it.

3. My goal is to eat healthier. That's why I want to stop before I eat this whole bag of chips!

4. I want to get rid of my credit card debt, so I can feel financially secure again.

5. I want to control my cravings so I can lose these love handles.

Answers: (1) Desired Outcome, Problem (2) Problem (3) Desired Outcome, Remedy (4) Remedy, Desired Outcome (5) Remedy, Remedy

2.4 *Activity*

How many words/phrases can you think of that a client might use to express a desire? There aren't all that many, actually. Take a few minutes to brainstorm a list of them, so you will be more apt to notice them when your client expresses a desired outcome. A thesaurus might come in handy!

1. I want...
2. I desire...
3. I wish...
4.
5.
6.
7.
8.

That's the *Want* Word, But...

Suppose your client comes up with a desired outcome like this:

Client: *The girls at school constantly put me down. (Problem)*

Facilitator: And the girls at school constantly put you down. And when girls constantly put you down, what would you like to have happen?

Client: *I want to punch out their lights! (Desired Outcome)*

Now, you might feel this is an appropriate time to stop the Symbolic Modeling process and remind your client about school rules or brainstorm options other than violence or even have them breathe deeply. You could use any number of other approaches you have honed as a professional. But are they based on an *assumption on your part* of what your client needs right now? You could be taking the session out of their hands, and inserting yourself as the expert.

Or you could stick with the SyM process. Respect that the client is the expert on themselves and on what they need now. Respect that *this is an opportunity for their system to learn from itself.* It is possible this client's "solution" is only a step they have come up with so far towards a yet-unidentified desired outcome. Don't assume just because they have given this as an outcome that it's all they know about what they want or how to get it. When you stay clean and just give them back their words, calmly and neutrally, along with CLQs, they are likely to come up with other realizations and solutions on their own.

Such an approach has many advantages. To name a few:

1. The solution won't be imposed by you.

2. The solution will be informed by the wisdom of your client's system.

3. Your client will be learning to work things out for themselves.

4. You will avoid triggering defensiveness.

You could ask, "And is there anything *else* you would like to have happen, when the girls put you down?" And you could keep repeating it and repeating it as they notice more about what they want and know.

Or you could respond with the remedy question (*Then what happens?*) to help them consider the possible consequences of their suggested want(s). Maybe punching the girls out is just what they want...and maybe there could be consequences they have not considered fully. Before they invest heavily in developing this desired outcome, they will do well to check into the consequences first.

Or the client may reveal other desired outcomes they are seeking:

Facilitator: And when you punch out their lights, then what happens?

Client: *Yeah. Maybe then I can relax and pay attention in class. I'd like that!*

> *Avoid offering premature solutions.*

As they explore these new desired outcomes further, their new focus might shift from the "girls putting me down" situation. Or not. What you have is an increasingly complex landscape with multiple problems and outcomes. Your client may know more about what's involved and needed than you might assume. A Symbolic Modeling session offers them an opportunity to explore the complexities and possibilities of their situation. And following the process will discourage you from offering premature solutions. Is there room for teaching deep breathing for relaxation? Other techniques or information? Sure. But you need not interrupt your Symbolic Modeling session. Let your client's subconscious lead the way with this experiential process, and they are likely to teach themselves much of what they need to know.

You don't work with adolescents? It is not hard to imagine an example similar to this with couples, say, or some work place situations. Clients may come up with remedies or outcomes that would clearly be detrimental to them or others in some important way.

> *You don't have to enable a clearly inappropriate outcome.*

And if their outcome, after much exploration and consideration, is something you as a therapist or coach can't condone, such as "punching someone's lights out," what then? At this point you can break from the modeling and conversationally address your client. You can make it clear you will not support working towards that behavior and give them the option of finding another professional to work with, with your assistance if they would like it. You don't have to enable a clearly inappropriate outcome!

Note: I am referring to outcomes acted out in the world, not to the client's metaphor landscape. It is not your role to determine what is appropriate there. And you can't assume a suggested action, like punching someone, means the client literally would or even wants to punch the actual person. You are working in metaphor, after all!

2.5 *Activity*

You will need a partner for this activity. Each of you will take a turn being a "challenging" client. The client's task is to answer every question with a **Problem** or a **Remedy** every time. Keep going until you mistakenly answer with a desired outcome. (It is harder than it sounds for most people to *not* give a desired outcome when asked the appropriate CLQ! If you are not already convinced, I think this activity will demonstrate for you the value of using these seemingly simple questions with your clients.) Switch roles when the client stumbles and states a desired outcome.

Reply to a Problem: "**And when** [x problem], **what would you like to have happen?**"

Reply to a Remedy: "**And when** [x problem is solved], **then what happens?**"

Example:

Facilitator: And what would you like to have happen?

Client: *I'm sick and tired of cleaning up after my spouse!*

Facilitator: And you're sick and tired of cleaning up after your spouse. And when sick and tired, what would you like to have happen?

Client: *It's been like this for years! Who does he think I am, his maid? I want to stop being taken for granted.*

Facilitator: And you're sick and tired of cleaning up after him. And it's been like this for years. And you want to stop being taken for granted. And when you're not taken for granted, then what happens?

Client: *I guess I've become a real nag, but it's so disrespectful to make me live in that mess! I'm so frustrated!!*

Facilitator: And you're so frustrated! And it's disrespectful. And when frustrated and it's disrespectful, what would you like to have happen?

When you are with a real client who sounds like this, they are not being difficult or resistant. They are revealing their pattern of behavior and thinking as it plays out right in front of you.

One approach you can use in this circumstance is to do what you did in the exercise above: continue repeating words and asking your P/R/O questions. Eventually, the client may shift their focus and explore what they know about their desired outcome.

A second approach is to slightly change your question and emphasis by asking, "And [x and y and z]. And when that's what you *don't* want, what *would* you like to have happen?"

Thirdly, after repeatedly coming back with a Problem when asked for a Desired Outcome, you can "go live" in the moment and explore the pattern itself by asking, "And what happens just after you are asked, "What would you like to have happen?"" The client can begin working on revising their processing rather than continuing the same frustrating pattern for years to come.

Metaphors' Desired Outcomes Revisited

You need to consider both your client's desired outcomes and those of the metaphors. It is important to be thinking of the whole of the landscape/client's system, and consider the relationship between *all* these desired outcomes.

If the client's and metaphors' *desired outcomes are in alignment*, they can strengthen and support one another so resources can be enhanced and momentum that energizes change can build. If the metaphors and/or the client have *conflicting desired outcomes*, these will need to be resolved, so that they will not be working against one another's interests.

Listen particularly for words about a metaphor that imply some kind of person-hood, intention, or ability to act or choose. (I start capitalizing such metaphors in my notes to remind me of their agency. Give it a try.)

Example:

Client: *There's a river that's trying to pick its way among the rocks. It's having a hard time.*

Facilitator: And a River, and trying to pick its way among the rocks. And when River is having a hard time, what would River like to have happen?

Client: *River would like my help.*

Facilitator: And River would like your help. And what kind of help is that help?

Client: *River wants me to get in. Somehow that would help it get around the rocks. Oh! I see. River wants me to move some of the rocks.*

Facilitator: And when River would like you to get in and move some of the rocks, what would *you* like to have happen?

When you explore the desires and needs of metaphors in the landscape as well as those of the client's:

- Relationships among symbols and the self are better understood
- Problems and/or desired changes may be revealed
- Help or encouraging permission may be given
- All the shareholders' needs and wants are considered, so the solution is more comprehensive and relapse is less likely.

While the exact question will depend on the order in which the information presents itself, the *concept* is basically:

> **"And when you want** [abc], **what would** [symbol x] **like to have happen?"**
>
> **"And when** [symbol x] **wants** [efg], **what would you like to have happen?"**

Aligned Desired Outcomes

It can be very encouraging to your client to discover that both their own and their symbols' desired outcomes can coexist and, perhaps, even reinforce one another.

Example continued:

Client: *I'd like to help River, but it looks too cold!*

Facilitator: And you'd like to help River. And it looks too cold. And when you'd like to help and it looks too cold, then what happens?

Client: *Oh, River's assuring me it will keep me warm enough. It can't move the rocks, but it can keep me warm enough, and it's happy to do that.*

Facilitator: And River assures you it will keep you warm enough. And you'd like to help River. And then what happens?

Client: *Then I know I'm loved, and I can love in return, and I'll help River. I'll move the rocks, if they'll cooperate.*

Conflicting Desired Outcomes

But sometimes, the symbol's desired outcome is different than your client's or another metaphor's. *If you don't address it, you could be leaving a symbol in the landscape working against the client's progress towards change.* Even if it seems beneficial, change can be hard; sticking with the familiar may be more comfortable for symbols, just like for people.

Let's consider several ways you could handle this conflict. Start by **reviewing** the two opposing desires for the client. Then, you could choose to ask one or both of these CLQs:

You could explore the consequences by asking:

> "[review]..., **then what happens?"**

Or since having desired outcomes in conflict presents a *problem*, you could ask:

> "[review]..., **what would you like to have happen?"**

Example continued:

Facilitator: And River wants you to move the Rocks. And you feel loved and can love in return, and you'll move the rocks, if they'll cooperate. And what would Rocks like to have happen?

Client: *The Rocks don't want me to move them.*

Facilitator: And the Rocks don't want you to move them. And when Rocks, what kind of Rocks are those Rocks?

Client: *These Rocks love the feeling of being caressed by the River as it goes over them.*

Facilitator: And River would like you to move them and you want to help River, and Rocks don't want you to move them; they love the feeling of being caressed. And then what happens?

Client: *The Rocks want to stay right where they are. They feel loved, and it's familiar and safe, and they don't want anything to change.*

Facilitator: And when Rocks don't want to move and River wants you to move them, what would you like to have happen?

Client: *I don't want to upset the Rocks. I'd like the River to talk to the Rocks, to reassure them, too.*

You can imagine that, if you hadn't discovered this problem, the Rocks might not have cooperated with the client's moving them at the River's request. With what I call the *dream logic* of metaphor landscape at work, where who knows what wisdom or desire these metaphors encode, the Rocks might have been moved, only to move right back into place a few minutes or days later. Or they may have been too heavy to move in the first place... or who knows what. We will get to what to do when something needs to change in the metaphor landscape in Section Four. For now, let this serve as a reminder to gather information about metaphors' desired outcomes, too, when you think P/R/O.

2.6 *Activity*

Practice asking for desired outcomes of symbols, especially those that have some sort of "it-ness," personification, agency, or intention. Use the full, three-part CL syntax so you can practice making choices about what and how much to repeat and giving yourself a bit of extra time to decide what you will ask.

1. I'm in a pasture. There's a menacing bull in the field with me. We're surrounded by a mean-looking fence, but I see a gate beckoning me.

2. There's a guard at attention just behind my eyes. It feels like he's been there a very long time. He's got a strong sense of duty, like he's been taking orders, and he would never question following them.

3. There's an energy that encircles me, that slowly spirals around me. I wish it would speed up or maybe get thicker. It doesn't seem to be paying attention to what I need.

4. There's a closet that's hiding all my treasures, all my deepest secrets. Sometimes when I try to open it, it's locked; other times it's open. It's got an unusual lock plate on it, swirly, almost like a face.

More About Explanations

Recall our **REPRO**Cess model, where the **E** stands for **E**xplanation. When you are busy concentrating on P/R/O, it can be easy to mislabel an explanation and make an assumption because of something hinted at. Listen carefully: an explanation may suggest a problem, a remedy, or a desired outcome, but you can't be sure without checking.

Remember to help your client get clear on what they want.

Example #1:

Client: *I've never been to Australia. My best friend says I'm missing out on a lot.*

Facilitator: And when you've never been to Australia and your best friend says you're missing out on a lot, what would *you* like to have happen?

Read carefully, and you will note this client has not actually said what they want. What they say is merely an **explanation** of the way things are. Maybe they have no desire to go to Australia! Maybe they don't see it as a problem. If you hear a statement like this, and it is unclear if there is a problem or desired outcome, check by using your CLQ to establish intention.

Consider the nuance in this next client statement.

Example #2:

Client: *Years ago, I wanted to go to Australia, but I couldn't afford it.*

Careful! A desired outcome refers to a *future want*, not to the past. You will have to update this explanation with an old want, check to see if it is still alive.

Example continued:

Facilitator: And when years ago you wanted to go to Australia but you couldn't afford it, what would you like to have happen now?

How about this next client statement?

Example #3:

Client: *I wanted to go to Australia for years, but I can't afford it.*

Facilitator: And when you wanted to go to Australia and you can't afford it, what would you like to have happen?

Pay close attention to verb tenses. Notice here, the want is in the past tense, "wanted", while "can't afford" is in the present tense. It's not uncommon for clients to do this sort of mixing and shifting, often unaware they've done it. Is this situation currently problematic for the client? Is there a desired outcome for the future in this statement? It is a bit iffy; the two verb tenses could suggest the client felt this way in the past and still does. Or it could suggest that the client has abandoned the idea with the realization they can't afford the trip; perhaps they have replaced it with an alternative. If the current desire is not crystal clear, you don't want head down a dead-end alley chasing an **E**xplanation. Simply ask the Desired Outcome question to get off on a proper start.

A facilitator lead astray by an assumption about the client's desires could easily begin to lead the session rather than letting the client's content lead.

Example #4:

Client: *If I could present my marketing ideas clearly at the next meeting, I think that could convince my boss I deserve that promotion.* *(Explanation)*

Facilitator: And present your ideas clearly and convince your boss, and deserve promotion. And when all that, what would you like to have happen? (Clarify D.O)

Client:	*You know, I give up hoping she'll notice!* *I'd like* ***to get up the courage*** *to sit down with* *my boss and* ***directly address*** *my promotion.* *Fact is, I feel good about my marketing ideas* *and my presentations to the team.* *What I need is to* ***be clear to her*** *about my* *career ambitions and my timeline. Then maybe she* *can spell out what I need to do to make that happen.*	***(Clear D.O.s,*** *Explanations)*

Example #5

Client:	*I grew up in the city where there were no pools,* *so I never learned to swim.*	*(Explanation)*
Facilitator:	And when you never learned to swim, what would you like to have happen?	(Clarify a D.O.)
Client:	*I sort of want to learn how to swim,* *but it's too late at my age to learn.*	*(Iffy D.O., Explanation)*
Facilitator:	And when you sort of want to learn how to swim, what kind of sort of is that sort of?	(Develop a D.O.)
Client:	*I do want to learn, but I'm too* *embarrassed to take a class.*	*(D.O., P)*
Facilitator:	And when you do want to learn to swim and you're too embarrassed to take a class, what would you like to have happen?	(Clarify D.O.)
Client:	*Listen to me?! I was operating under some belief* *that I couldn't learn, wasn't allowed to at my age,* *somehow. I'm stopping myself! I'm not going to* *let embarrassment stop me! My sister knows how* *to swim, and she's not judgmental. I'll get her to teach me.*	*(Explanations, D.O.)*

Some explanations are not helpful. Others may be relevant to your client's desired outcomes, for embedded in them are *implied* desired outcome(s) or problem(s) related to your client's way of processing, to how they see the world and manage it. With CLQs, you can help your client take an explanation into a clearly-stated desired outcome and/or reveal a previously unstated problem.

2.7 Activity

The following client statements are broken into parts below. Identify them as **E**xplanations, **P**roblems, **R**emedies, or **O**utcomes.

Client: *My father was not a demonstrative person. I wish he hadn't been so cold. He never hugged us as children. I struggle to this day to express affection to my boy, even though it's important to me that he know how much I love him. I know my father did the best he could. I'd like to feel less angry about what's in the past and accept him for who he is.*

____ 1. My father was not a demonstrative person.

____ 2. I wish he hadn't been so cold.

____ 3. He never hugged us as children.

____ 4(a). I struggle to this day to express affection to my boy,...

____ 4(b). ...even though it's important to me that he know how much I love him.

____ 5. I know my father did the best he could.

____ 6(a). I'd like to feel less angry about what's in the past…

____ 6(b). ...and accept him for who he is.

Answers: 1) E 2) E (in the past) 3) E 4a) P 4b) D.O. 5) E 6a) R 6b) D.O.

Separating the Wheat from the Chaff with Metaphor

How can you, as the facilitator, help your client determine what is useful or relevant to addressing their issue and what is not? You can't always depend upon your client to know, even with the desired outcome question. The information may simply not be available to your client's conscious awareness. Nor can you, whatever your experience and expertise, know. This is why it is so useful to go into metaphor; your client's subconscious sorts it out for you both. Get a metaphor for your client's desired outcome, and the deeper truth will emerge.

It is common for clients to start off their sessions by giving you background information, full of explanations. In fact, they can use up a lot of your time together giving you information that is not particularly helpful. Don't get distracted by what happened historically in the past or by what the client reports someone else says or does.

Recall the quote from psychotherapist Virginia Satir that starts this Section: "The problem is not the problem; coping is the problem." How is the client processing their experience now? What do they want to have happen? What can you help with, right here and now, so they leave with something that is useful to them? Note that the answer needn't be tangible or overtly practical; it could be to be more in touch with their own knowing or to have a greater felt sense of their own inner calm or strength. As you clarify their desired outcomes, you trust your client's wisdom as to what they need in the moment.

REPROCess Purpose

Think REPROCess and get into metaphor! Once you master the process, you will use P/R/O and Explanations to think about consequences, goals, and what might be unspoken between the lines. These insights will guide your questioning, and that is the ultimate purpose of the REPROCess model.

2.8 *Activity*

These next client statements are more like real-life client ones, and they are challenging. It can feel like there is a lot coming at you all at once! Thinking **REPRO-** helps you sort it out. What part of each statement here is **E**xplanation? Does the client have a **D**esired **O**utcome? Do you see an opportunity to get a metaphor for a **R**esource? Where would you start? Plan a strategy for each passage as to what you would likely direct attention towards and what questions you would ask. Discuss your choices with your practice buddy. (Naturally, once you actually start with a real client, your choices after your first question or two could—most likely, would— change, depending on the information that emerges. This exercise is for practice.)

1. I've held my current job for 14 years. I've risen through the ranks alright, sort of right on schedule. I'm the vice president in charge of East Coast sales now. The thing is, my bosses want me to move to Chicago, and I don't want to move. Chicago is cold in winter, and it's far from my family in Florida. But I want to keep growing my career. What if my company no longer see me as a go-getter?

2. I am the middle child in my family. My brother, Peter, is an engineer with NASA. He's 3 years older than me. Mom and Dad were always so proud of him! It was tough for me to get their attention. I was the shy one. Still am, sometimes. There are times I want to come out of my shell, but I just can't seem to, especially if my brother is around. It's like there's a perpetual spotlight on him. My sister isn't shy either. She was a cheerleader, really outgoing, still is. It's not that I want the kind of attention they thrive on; I'd just like to feel seen without having to be loud about it and without feeling like I have to compete for attention. I'm not a competitive kind of person. Even as a kid, I never wanted to be on a competitive team.

3. My son, Jason, is applying to colleges for next fall. This has been a real source of tension in the family, and I want to ease things for us all. I mean, this is important, but so are our relationships! I remember when I was applying for college. I was so much more interested in basketball that I sort of blew the whole thing off. Good thing my dad practically held my head under water to force me to send my application to our state university. Me, I'm not like my dad. I've been leaving this whole college thing up to my wife to handle, and she's constantly on my case about it.

4. I've always been a pack-rat. I think it comes with being a teacher, you know? Never know when something might come in handy again, you know? And we're always hard up for supplies at school. "Waste not, want not," they say, right? But I do find a great sense of relief when I toss things out, like I'm unburdening myself. Then I worry maybe I'll need those things, so I put half the stuff back in boxes at the back of the closet. And we're short on closet space! Do you do this sort of thing?

5. I just got back from spending the holidays with dad. I'm worried about him. He went out to buy some cigarettes and was gone for, like, an hour. Turns out he got lost on the way home! His wife, my step-mother, died about 6 months ago, and I know it's been hard on him... for him. Maybe he just got distracted. But, I mean, should he live alone? Is that even my business to be making that call? There's a part of me that wants to respect his autonomy and let him make his own decisions. I wouldn't want anyone telling me where and how to live.

2.9 *Activity*

Time again to practice with a partner. But first, take a moment to look back at what you wrote in activity 1.5. What was it you wanted to work on from that practice session? Still need to work on them? Have others to add? List them together here. As you practice facilitating this time, make a point of working on a few of these. Plan on 30 minutes each. You may want to use the chart on the next page.

My goals for this practice session:

Then answer the following questions:

Something I did well was:

Something I want to work on next time is:

CHART: Developing A Desired Outcome Landscape

DEVELOPING A DESIRED OUTCOME LANDSCAPE

1. Establish a clear Desired Outcome using P/R/O.

Problem	And what would you like to have happen?
Remedy	And when [reworded remedy], then what happens?

2. Develop the Desired Outcome:

Metaphor	And that's like... what?
Attributes	What kind of/Anything else about that [x]?
Location	And whereabouts is that [x]?
Time	And what happens just before/after?
Relationship	And when [x] and [y], is there a relationship between that [x] and that [y]?
Source	And where could [x] come from?

3. Follow the same steps for any additional Problems, Remedies, and Desired Outcomes that emerge.

Section Two Summary

REPROCess: An acronym for the things your client is attending to. Helps you determine what to direct your client's attention towards or away from. (R) Resources, (E) Explanations, (P) Problem, (R) Remedy, (O) Desired Outcome, (C) Change, and -ess for its part in *reprocessing*. REPROCess guides *your* navigating; it does not dictate outcomes for your client.

Resources are those things that have value *to your clien*t because they are helpful to them in some way. Resources may be **overt**, **latent**, or **to-be-converted**. The **source of a resource** is often more useful and/or powerful than the resource itself.

Problems, remedies, and outcomes are not always neatly identified or sequential. Use **P/R/O modeling** as a way to think about consequences, goals, and what might be unspoken between the lines to guide your questioning.

Determine whether the client and their metaphors have **desired outcomes** that are **aligned** or in **conflict**.

Explanations can be relevant to your client's desired outcomes. Listen closely for possible implied problems or desired outcomes *related to their processing*.

Explanations can also be distractions. By getting into metaphor, you enable the client's subconscious to sort out what is truly relevant to achieving their desired outcomes.

My take-away from this section is...

Questions I have...

2.10 *Activity*

Begin by determining whether these statements are Problems, Remedies, and/or Desired Outcomes (There will be Explanations in these, too, but concentrate on P/R/O!). Repeating all three parts of the full syntax **out loud**, respond with an appropriate CLQ . (These questions need to be as fluid coming out of your mouth as they sound in your head.) Use the time while you are saying lines one and two to decide exactly which CLQ you will ask, which is what you can do with an actual client to keep the flow of the session steady.

CLQs in response to a:

Problem: **"And** [x]**. And when** [x]**, what would you like to have happen?"**

Remedy: **"And** [x]**. And when** [reworded statement removing problem]**, then what happens?**

Desired Outcome: **"And** [x]**. And when** [x]**, what kind of** [x] **is that** [x]**?"**

"And when [x]**, is there anything else about that** [x]**?"**

or another developing CLQ

1. I feel like my very foundation has been undermined.

2. I want to send his negativity away from me!

3. I want to attract a good partner into my life.

4. I'd like to reduce the number of headaches I get to no more than 1 or 2 a month.

5. I can't foresee my child's teacher and me ever seeing eye-to-eye, but we need to find a way to work together despite our differences.

6. I hope I can put my best foot forward in the next round of interviews.

7. I don't want to disappoint my mother, but, then again, she's never satisfied.

8. I've been laid off twice in the last 3 years due to the tailspin the economy's been in, so I'm determined to go into business for myself to have more job security.

9. I want a ritual of some sort so I can quit procrastinating about starting my work.

10. There isn't a new boat in the harbor that's interesting enough that I'm willing to get on the new one and leave the old boat. The old boat is covered with barnacles; it needs work. I'm not sure I really want to put that kind of work into an old boat, though. I could work and work, and it would still be an old boat.

11. I always feel driven, like a freight train, rumbling forward, unable to stop, even though I'm exhausted. Got to keep moving! Got a schedule to keep! Places to go! Things to deliver! I'm like the Little Engine That Could.

12. There is music playing in my head. Sometimes it is loud, and sometimes it is soft. It is always there to soothe and inspire me. It sounds like harps playing. It's a nice sound that feels familiar in an ancient sort of way.

Answers: (1) Problem (2) Remedy (3) Desired Outcome (4) Remedy (5) Problem and Desired Outcome (6) Desired Outcome (7) Remedy and an Implied Problem (Explanation) (8) Implied Problem (Explanation) and Desired Outcome (9) Desired Outcome and a Remedy (10) Problem (11) Problem (12) Explanation

Want More Practice?

You can re-purpose many of the examples in the activities in this workbook for practicing other questions or Clean strategies other than what the directions call for. We are getting ready to add new CLQs in the next section, so if there is something you need more practice with, now is a good time to do it.

Section Three

"Yet the stones remain less real to those who cannot
name them, or read the mute syllables graven in silica.
To see a red stone is less than seeing it as jasper—
metamorphic quartz, cousin to the flint the Kiowa
carved as arrowheads. To name is to know and remember."

-Dana Gioia

SPECIALIZED QUESTIONS

Depending on how confident you are with the basic nine CLQs we have covered so far, you may or may not be glad to hear that there are other Clean questions that are commonly used that fall outside the parameters of the SyM Frameworks for Change basics. I snuck a few into *Basics Part One*. Here we will add considerably more. Like the others, they are all simple, open-ended, and clean of the facilitator's content.

Before you get excited and think I am going to turn you loose, wait up! There is a good reason the nine questions we have covered are called basic questions: you really should be using them most of the time. The fewer questions you use, the more predictable what you say becomes and the less your client has to cognitively process what you are asking. They are able to stay focused on *their* material and not get distracted deciphering what you are asking.

But sometimes a little flexibility is a good thing. Symbolic Modeling embraces what we call specialized questions[1] that are useful for developing specific sorts of details. The basic rule of thumb: follow your client's logic. *Seek to ask a question it seems likely your client already has, or can easily get, an answer to.* Don't go on a fishing expedition. Sometimes, your client is just discovering a metaphor; it is as if their camera has zoomed in, but the symbol is not in focus yet. These specialized questions direct your client's attention to some of the details very likely to emerge.

Expand Your Repertoire Gradually

The goal with these specialized questions is not to add them all to your modeling right away. Pick a few that appeal to you, practice using them until they become natural and automatic, then add a few more, and repeat. They are meant to help you, not overwhelm you!

Specialized Attribute Questions

An often-used specialized question you might start with is:

> **"And does that [x] have a *size* or a *shape*?"**

Example:

Client: *I have this determination in my gut. It's always served me when I needed it. Without it, I don't know how I'd have passed the bar exam.*

Facilitator: And determination, in your gut, and it's always served you. And when determination in your gut, does that determination have a size or shape?

Notice that I have asked this size/shape question of a word that the client has described as an *it* that *serves*, suggesting it might be an embedded metaphor, and that they are already aware of its location. If it is an object/thing, it follows logically that it could have a size or shape. You will notice, too, that the Clean Language Question is not, "*What is* [x]'s size or shape?", but *does it have* a size or shape? It is important that the phrase and your tone do not suggest that there is or even should be either; you are just inviting your client to observe. Likewise, *size* and *shape* are paired together, not asked for separately. To ask for both at the same time

subtly reinforces the sense that you are just inviting your client to notice possible new information.

Deconstructing this specialized question gives you a good idea of how very carefully David Grove designed these Clean Language Questions, and why it is important to keep to their exact wording.

Specifying Size

Speaking of size, this specialized question can really focus the client's attention on this detail. You can use it to encourage a more embodied experience or clarify its scale in relation to other symbols in the landscape. Note that it, too, gives two options.

> **"And when** [x], **how *big* or how *small* could that** [x] **be?"**

Specifying Quantity

Another useful specialized attribute question to help your client bring what can be a significant detail into focus is:

> **"And how *many*** [x's] **could there be?"**

Example:

Client: *Lots of people have come to greet me.*

Facilitator: And lots of people have come to greet you. And when lots of people, how many people could there be?

For the client, knowing whether there are 5 or 6 people or 50-60 is often quite significant. If "lots" turns out to be "5 or 6," and I realize that I was thinking 50 or 60, it is an excellent reminder of how very easy it is to make assumptions. Sometimes, I haven't even realized I had a number in mind until I find I am surprised!

One of the gifts of learning Clean Language is how much more aware you become of the subtle and not so subtle assumptions we all routinely make. It is why getting clarity is so important for you and for the client--for they, too, may have made inaccurate assumptions.

Making the Most of "More"

Clients often express a desire for more of something valuable or helpful. Helping a client discover how much of a resource they currently have and how much more they want can clarify what was vague and make more manageable what was daunting. The exact phrasing will differ depending on the client's exact words and the context, but essentially you can ask one or both of these questions:

> **"And when you** [want more x], **how much** [x] **do you have now?"**

> **"And when you** [want more x], **how much more** [x] **do you want?"**

Example:

Client: *I want more clients; I need to expand my practice.*

Facilitator: And expand your practice. And more clients. And when more clients, how many more clients do you want?

Client: *Enough to cover my expenses and have some left over, for sure. But I don't want to be overwhelmed so much so that I can't do a good job.*

Facilitator: And when cover your expenses and some left over and not overwhelmed, is there anything else about how many more clients you want?

Client: *I can handle about two more a day, say 8-10 more per week. Yes, that would be good. Huh, when I put it like that, it doesn't seem so hard.*

More Inner Resources

Getting clarity and specificity about an inner resource can also be very helpful. Logically, if a client wants more of something, they must have some already. It is sometimes a surprise to a client to realize they do have some courage or relaxation or whatever, and it is a resource they can build on. Help them find their metaphor for it. That will help bring into focus how much more [x] they want and what would happen then. You can then develop the resource metaphor's other attributes, so your client can know it well and be able to locate it in the future.

Example:

Client: *I wish I could be more resilient.*

Facilitator: And more resilient. And when resilient, that's resilient like what?

Client: *Resilient like jumping on a trampoline. I'd just keep bouncing back up, higher than I go now.*

Facilitator: And bouncing back up. And when bouncing, how high do you go now?

Client: *Hardly at all, so it takes a lot of effort to keep bouncing.*

Facilitator: And now you bounce back up hardly at all. And how high would you like to bounce back up?

Client: *I could bounce back about 2 feet. I'm bouncing enough to keep my momentum going easily, yet I'm still in control.*

Did you notice the shift in the client's verb tense in that last statement? The client starts by describing what they could do, and then they talk about what they are doing, as if it is happening now. Change can happen spontaneously just with greater clarity and exploration!

Specialized Location Questions

Recall that when you learned the CLQ, "And where/whereabouts is that [x]?", I encouraged you to ask the question several times. Your client often gets surprising and helpful information by getting more and more specific about just where something is.

Here are some specialized CLQs to help your client locate precisely.

#1 In Reference to the Body

"And where could that [x] **be: on the *inside*? on the *outside*?"**

Example:

Facilitator: And confidence like a sphere of energy. And when a sphere of energy, **whereabouts** is that sphere?

Pause here and wait patiently. If your client really struggles for an answer, you can add:

Facilitator: **"On the inside? On the outside?"**

#2 The Space Between

"And when [x] **is there,... and when** [y] **is there, ... what's *between* that** [x] **and that** [y]**?**

Example:

Facilitator: And the gold ring you want is right there in front of you. And when you are there, and gold cup is there, what's between you and that cup?

#3 Direction of Movement

"And in which *direction* is/does [x move]**?"**

Example:

Facilitator: And a pinwheel, in your gut, spinning. And when in your gut and spinning, in which direction is that pinwheel spinning?

#4 Locating the client

Sometimes your client makes it clear that they are in their landscape, but you are not sure precisely where they are. You can ask:

"And whereabouts are *you*?"

They may be very aware, and the answer simply helps you better determine what questions to ask. Or it may be they are so wrapped up in exploring other aspects of the landscape that they haven't noticed their location. Where they are in relationship to other symbols can make them aware of new perspectives, possibilities, or problems.

Example:

Client: *There's a bonfire there and trees all around it, hiding it from view.*

Facilitator: And when there's a bonfire and trees hiding it from view, where are you?

Client: *I'm above it, looking down. I have a bird's-eye view. Huh! Wonder what I'm doing up here? I can see beyond the trees.*

#5 Distance

Distance can hold a lot of meaning metaphorically, often relating to accessibility, safety, a sense of connection, and the time it takes to accomplish or connect with [x]. I find clients are often surprised by the answer they discover to this question:

"And when [x]**, how *near* or how *far* could that** [x] **be?"**

Example:

Facilitator: And when your goal is in front of you, how near or how far in front?

Client: *Just out of reach. Huh! Closer than I realized... just barely out of reach.*

Specialized Time Question

You may notice this next question is also listed as a location question. Since we describe time in terms of space (the past is behind us, the future lies ahead, etc.), the same question we use for *locating* can be used for *sequencing* purposes: to draw the client's attention to what happens between occurrences. Although you can use this question when you are exploring small gaps in time, the same as you can use the after-and-before question (Section One), I tend to use this question in circumstances in which the events are further apart in time. It is your choice.

"And what's *between* [x happening] **and** [y happening]**?"**

Example:

Facilitator: And when you start off some days feeling great and by noon you feel a headache coming on, what's between that feeling great and that headache?

Client: *I read the newspaper, and then I start feeling overwhelmed and helpless.*

Specialized Relationship Questions

Sometimes your client repeats a word several minutes apart, but something about it the second time makes you think it might be different from the previous mention of it. Other times, you may simply want to encourage your client to explore similarities and/or differences. You can ask:

> **"And is that the *same*** [x] **or a *different*** [x] **than** [previously mentioned x]**?"**

> **"And is that the *same as or different from*** [y]**?"**

Don't worry about it sounding grammatically logical; with Clean Language's syntax or phrasing, it may not. It won't bother your client. What's important is that it makes sense within the logic of your client's landscape.

Examples:

Facilitator: And you're determined to get out of the tunnel. And you're determined to get on with your life. And is that determined to get out of the tunnel and that determined to get on with your life the same determined or a different determined?

Client: *Oh, they're different! The determined to get out of the tunnel is forceful, like rushing, turbulent water. The determined to get on with my life...is like a dripping faucet; it's consistent, it's persistent, but it's so small... too small!*

3.1 Activity

Practice writing and asking aloud at least two specialized questions of the following statements. There's a chart of all the specialized questions further on in this Section. For this activity, just use the ones in the first four categories: attributes, location, time, and relationship.

1. I am on a beach, and there are lots of crabs scurrying around, some red and some greenish-brown. I want to get them back to the ocean, but they can't get there.

2. Confidence is in my chest, above my heart. And I can hold it, but then it dissipates and moves away from me.

3. I want to be more connected to my intuition, maybe have several connections, that could be different sizes and go in different directions.

4. There are all these people on a stage, and they are getting ready to perform. I want to join them. I need to make the leap, to get from watching to being one of them. I would feel welcomed and accepted.

5. I hear a buzzing sound behind me and then a buzzing in front of me. It's hard to be patient, but it's absolutely necessary. And then I'm off, running as fast as I can.

6. There's this warmth in my heart that's at the very core of me. It needs more oxygen, a steady supply. My blood carries oxygen, but it's not getting enough to where I need it most.

Specialized Review Questions

When you have collected a lot of information, and you want to draw your client's attention to *the whole*, you can ask:

> **"And** [review details]**.**
>
> **And is there anything else about *all that?*"**
> or
> **"And when all that,...**[relevant CLQ]**?"**

To zoom out and consider a larger whole, we can also borrow a clean question from David Grove's Clean Space technique that we touched on in *Basics Part One*. This question should be used when you are pretty confident from what's happening that your client has an answer. *The point is to help your client notice and articulate what they know, not send them off searching in the hopes that they will find something.*

> **"And when [review details], what difference does knowing all that make?"**

This 'what difference" is a question that may elicit a cognitive sort of answer, so you may want to save it for when you are wrapping up and moving the client from an inner-focused state back to a more outwardly-focused state of normal interaction and conversation. The question provides a natural segue to planning, for taking what was learned in the session into conscious decisions, choices, and actions. Remember, however, that some clients will still be in a slightly fuzzy, still-processing-all-this mode, and may not want to get analytical. Honor that internal shifts may still be occurring, and your client may need to do such planning at another time or, at least, after a break.

Other Specialized Questions

#1 In the Moment

After a client's long pause, and you sense something has been going on (perhaps a change in facial expression or shifting around), you might ask gently, not demandingly:

"And what's happening?" or **"And what just happened?"**

This is also a good way to reference an emotional response your client is having in the moment, to which they haven't put any words. It brings attention to the here-and-now.

Example:

Facilitator: (Noticing the client has teared up) And what's happening?

Client: *I just feel such love from River. It feels so unconditional, so timeless. Like it's always been there for me and always will be.*

#2 Encourage the client to choose

When there's a great deal of information, and you are stumped as to what to ask next, you can ask this beautifully open-ended question that invites your client to tap into their intuitive knowing and self-direct:

"And [review a sizable chunk of information]**.**
And when all that, what are you drawn to?

Note: *This should not be a default or cop-out question!* If you find yourself asking this often because you don't know what else to ask, slow down; give yourself time to decide on a more strategically-selected question.

#3 Mindful Knowing

I often find these to be surprisingly powerful specialized questions, further enhancing a client's mindful awareness of their thoughts, feelings, and/or body.

"And what do you know about that [x]**?"**
"And when [x]**, how do you know** [x]**?"**

Example:

Client: *I want to feel balanced.*

Facilitator: And balanced. And when feel balanced, how do you know you're balanced?

Client: *Well, my mind's stopped racing. I'm breathing more slowly and deeply, and I feel sort of calm, like I don't need to be doing anything other than just what I'm doing at that moment. I'm relaxed.*

#4 Choice Point

An excellent awareness to develop is for when your client is describing a *choice point*. This is often a moment when something occurs that keeps their present pattern repeating.

- It could be a good thing if their choice helps them maintain a resourceful state.
- It could be a problem if the pattern of thought, feeling, or behavior does not serve them well.

In either case, your client can use more information about a moment of choice. *It will help them strengthen the beneficial and learn how to go about changing the problematic.*

You can ask:

> **"And what determines whether you** [do x] **or** [do y]**?"**
> **"And what determines whether you** [do x] **or don't** [do x]**?"**

(Stay clean! Don't ask *why* they do [x]; it may put people on the defensive or get them analyzing.)

Example:

Client: *I can get motivated to go the extra mile at work; then again, I can get really resistant, too.*

Facilitator: And you can get motivated to go the extra mile. And you can get resistant. And when motivated at work, what determines whether you get motivated?

I have given you this example to remind you that you don't have to focus on the metaphor every time you use CLQs. By asking *what determines whether* the client is motivated or resistant, they may well stay focused on practical answers about what they do at work. I find this question, with its words *determines whether*, invites a more cognitive or analytical response as compared to the response elicited by a basic CLQ, which uses short, simple words. The question choice above might be appropriate in a context where you are using CLQs with everyday content, such as a business meeting.

If you were intending to focus on metaphors, you could start right off by learning more about that *extra mile*—getting the client solidly in their symbolic domain before exploring their motivation issues, so you could access and involve the deeper knowing of their subconscious mind/body. In that case, I would choose to use basic moving time questions to explore the metaphor landscape, rather than the *what determines whether* question, so as to encourage their trance state. But the intention remains the same: to figure out what determines this client's choices.

Example:

Facilitator: And motivated. And the extra mile. And is there anything else about that extra mile?

Client: *Yes, it's like a race. It seems daunting at first, but then I start, and I'm all in!*

Facilitator: And a race. And you start, and you're all in. And when race and daunting at first, what happens *after* it seems daunting and *before* you start?

You are looking to help your client identify problems and resources. Be careful not to jump to conclusions about what their resourceful state is! Remember—it depends on the individual context. Some clients may want more motivation to work; others may be driving themselves to exhaustion and want to stop always going the extra mile. Notice the client's initial statement is an **E**xplanation. The questions in this example will help them develop some contextual information so they can be clearer on what goes on for them, before you ask for their **D**esired **O**utcome:

Client: *I can get really resistant, like a pulling back... like reins pulling back.*

Facilitator: And when you can get motivated to go the extra mile and all in, and when you can get really resistant, like reins pulling back, what would you like to have happen?

Client: *I'd like to take that sense of resistance as a message that I am trying to do too much. I'd like to pay attention to it, rather than ignoring it.*

Facilitator: And sense of resistance as a message. And when a sense of resistance, like reins pulling back, whereabouts are those reins?

CHART: Specialized Questions

SPECIALIZED QUESTIONS

Attributes

And does that [x] have a size or shape?
And when [x], how big or small could that [x] be?
And when [x plural], how many [x's] could there be?
And when you [want more x], how much do you have now?
And when you [want more x], how much more [x] do you [want]?

Location

And where is that [x]: on the inside? on the outside?
And what's between that [x] and [y]?
And when [x movement], in which direction is/does [x movement]?
And when [x], how near or far is that [x]?

Time

And what's between [x happening] and [y happening]?

Relationship

And when [review], is there anything else about all that?
And [review]. And when all that, [a CLQ]?
And when [review], what difference does knowing all that make?

Others

And what's happening?/And what just happened?
And what are you drawn to?
And what do you know about [x]?
And when [x], how do you know [x]?
And what determines whether you [do x] or [do y]?

3.2 *Activity*

While a CL session is never strictly linear, the progression of 5 steps below for developing a resource is a good one to have in mind. Practice working with resources using CLQs, using your own paper for note-taking. If you are working with a practice buddy, you can alternate being client and facilitator. If you are on your own, switch hats! The client should keep their answers fairly short, so the facilitator can concentrate on the questions and their progression. Take your time; this is practice!

1) Identify a **resource** in the statement.
2) Develop some of the attributes of the resource with basic CLQs. (AE, WKO, WH)
3) Take the resource into **metaphor**. (TLW)
4) Develop some of the attributes of the resource metaphor with basic CLQs (AE, WKO, WH).
5) Further develop the resource metaphor with at least three **specialized** CLQs.

1. I want to be free from the inside out.

2. I want to be flexible about changing my work habits, now that I have a new boss.

3. I want to be more accepting of the pace at which I am releasing past hurts.

4. At the end of the day, I wish I could let go of work issues in my head and, when I get home, really relax and be more present!

5. I want to be more deeply aligned with my true purpose, the reason I was born.

6. I want to be more mindful of others' sensitivities.

7. I want to be more loving and forgiving of my aging parents' frailty and forgetfulness.

8. I want to be able to gather my inner fortitude when it's needed and bring it to bear.

3.3 *Activity*

Time for another client or partner practice. Try giving a full 30 minutes for each facilitator. You have a lot of questions and facilitating strategies to work with now. Decide which charts you need at your side for reference. Select a few specialized questions to try working into your facilitation, and make note of them here or add them to a chart.

I'd like to try using these specialized questions, if the opportunity arises:

1)

2)

3)

Afterwards, answer the following questions:

Something I did well was:

Something I want to work on next time is:

Creating Your Own Specialized Questions

We have covered about 20 common specialized questions, but this is not an exhaustive list. Once you get truly comfortable with Clean Language, there may be times you create your own specialized questions. Just remember:

- Keep them to a minimum. When you repeat the same basic questions,
    1. Your client doesn't need to engage in interpreting a multitude of different questions.
    2. The effects of your presence on your client's self-exploration are minimized.
    3. You help your client maintain their inner-focused state. It also offers your client a safe haven of a sort: they can let up staying prepared for surprise questions.
- Keep them clean.
- Avoid sounding too wordy or conversational; mimic the rhythmic, simple, even slightly awkward wording of the basic CLQs.
- Be true to the logic of your client's landscape.
- Have you noticed that no CLQ ever includes *why*? Asking for analysis takes the client out of their experience, and puts them into their heads. We are often not very accurate at knowing why we do things, anyway. In a Clean session, we are going for a different sort of knowing.

Examples:

Client: *There's a wall in front of me that's pretty high. I'd like to get over it, but I can't.*

A GOOD example:

Facilitator: And a wall in front and pretty high. And when high, how high could that wall be?

A BAD example:

Facilitator: And a wall in front and pretty high. And, if I understand you correctly, you can't conceivably get over it. And, in your experience, has anyone else ever gotten over a wall like that?

Why bad? It's not *clean*! A few reasons are:

- The question uses longer, multi-syllabic words (like experience and conceivably).
- It adds words unnecessarily that are not the client's.
- The facilitator refers to themselves (If I understand you...)
- The facilitator asks about other people whom the client has not introduced and whose ability to get over the wall may not be at all helpful or relevant.
- The same would be true if the facilitator were to ask if another symbol had gone over the wall; they would be "dirtying" the landscape with their own suggestion.

Section Three Summary

Specialized questions help draw your client's attention to more specific details. They should closely follow the logic of their landscape.

There is value in using mostly basic questions and few specialized questions. The fewer different questions you use, the more predictable they are, and the less your client has to cognitively process what you are asking.

Be on the lookout for **choice points**, when your client can choose to do things differently or keep an existing pattern repeating.

If and when you **create your own Clean Language questions**, be true to the rhythm, the spirit, and the intent of the basic and specialized questions. Stay clean!

My take-away from this section is...

Questions I have...

3.4 *Activity*

Practice asking **three specialized questions** of the following statements. Focus on developing information primarily about desired outcomes and resource states. Refer to the previous chart. Then use these statements any other way you would like that will help you practice what you most want to practice.

1. What I need to know is that someone could call the fire department to send more people who can put out fires and administer emergency first aid, if I need them to.

2. It's like I've been walking a really long, long time, and I'm really thirsty and dirty, and then I hear a rushing sound nearby. I'm tired, but I am still determined.

3. There's this cocoon where I'm safe. But a part of me wants to come out now, so it can grow up. And a part of me wants to stay little and safe.

4. I don't know which I have more of, anger or grief. I don't want to get rid of either of them. I *should* be angry after what happened, and I *should* be sad! But I don't want to be overwhelmed by either of them. I want to control them rather than let them control me.

Section Four

*"It may be hard for an egg to turn into a bird;
it would be a jolly sight harder for it to learn to fly
while remaining an egg."*

-C.S. Lewis

The Clean Language developing questions you have learned so far have been for the purpose of clarifying what your client knows and uncovering new information. The time and relationship questions can take your client into actively and strategically working with that information. You move into yet another stage of the Symbolic Modeling process when your client expresses a desire for a change that hasn't unfolded spontaneously as a result of new awareness or clarity. This is Stage 4 of the Symbolic Modeling process. In this section, you will learn how you can help your client establish what conditions need to be met before their desired change can occur. It is easy to make assumptions regarding conditions and skip too lightly through this stage. Here you will discover just how important it is to take the time to thoroughly inquire about and explore these conditions in order for your client to make lasting and comprehensive change.

Readiness for Change

Notice—and this is important!!—it is the client who identifies what they want to change and when they are ready for it. It is not your job to fix things for the client or to determine what they should do or when they should do it. If giving advice and setting goals for your clients has been an important part of what you do, this different approach may be hard to accept. I encourage you to open yourself to this new way of thinking and working and give it a chance. You will still be an important part of your client's process, as you help facilitate their exploration of the hows and whens and whats of their change. You can assist your client in:

- Getting **clarity** on what they want
- Exploring possible **consequences**
- Sequencing the **steps** involved
- Overcoming **stumbling blocks**
- Building up the **motivation** and **momentum** to initiate and sustain change
- Developing needed **resources**, both external and internal
- Aligning needs, wants, and values for **comprehensive** change

You can direct attention to all these parts of the change process with your CLQs, exploring all that your client might need to consider before being able to leave behind an old way of behaving or believing or being, and adopting a new way. But, ultimately, you must respect your client's knowing of what change is right for them and when it happens.

As this course is an introduction to Symbolic Modeling, we will not delve into the more complex ways clients have for staying stuck nor how to deal with those patterns. What follows is how the process can facilitate the majority of issues for most people.

Metaphors Facilitate Change

Your client may declare they are ready, but the change they swear they are dying for just doesn't seem to happen or they can't maintain the change. Such examples are why working with metaphors can be so helpful, for they reveal what your client may not know.

To expand on what we covered in Section One, *metaphors*...

- Bypass the conscious mind's tendency to filter what it's convinced can't possibly be changed or talked about or perhaps even admitted to its conscious self.
- Ignore what the client may consciously think is relevant, but isn't.
- Reveal the parts of the system the client may never have realized are relevant, exposing how the status quo both maintains blocks and provides rewards.

Ultimately, connecting with these guiding internal metaphors in a non-threatening way using Symbolic Modeling loosens up the system's current configuration and helps your client open to new possibilities. Sensorially and emotionally *experiencing* these desirable new possibilities encourages neuroplasticity or changes in the brain.[2] Thus, you can help facilitate substantive change with a Clean session.

Clean Language Questions #10 and #11: Conditions for Change

Once your client has clearly determined their desired outcome and developed an image of the symbol(s) involved, they will need to establish what else, if anything, needs to happen in order for the desired change to occur. These are called their *conditions for change*. I think of them as sub-desired outcomes, because the client presumably wants them, too, to achieve their desired outcome.

Establishing Conditions Questions

> **"And what needs to happen for** [D.O.]**?"**
>
> **"And is there anything else that needs to happen for** [D.O.]**?"**
>
> **"And can** [D.O.]**?"**

Example:

Facilitator: And there's a black iron bridge, about 20 feet long, there, 10 feet in front of you. And when a bridge, in front, what would you like to have happen ?

Client: *I'd like to go over it. The other side looks very inviting!*

Facilitator: And you'd like to go over it. And **what needs to happen** for you to go over that bridge?

Client: *The way is clear. There's nothing I can see blocking me.*

Facilitator: And **can you** go over that bridge?

Client: *Yes! I'm going over it now. The other side is getting closer and closer.*

Sometimes nothing else needs to happen. Just being aware of the symbols, with their attributes and locations, and identifying what they want to have happen is enough for your client's change to unfold. Most likely, if you have been working with clients or a practice partner or been a client yourself, this has happened. In a situation like this, you could move right on to Stage 5 of the process, maturing the change(s), which we will get to in Section Five.

Listing Conditions for Change

But other times, your client may have one or more (sometimes many more!) conditions that need to be met. Not only may there be four or five conditions, for example, but some of those conditions may have conditions, too, that need to be resolved. In this next example, you will notice two important rules of thumb when using these conditions for change questions:

1. You **keep reviewing** the client's conditions so they can hold the whole list in mind and the landscape remains psychoactive, though you need not repeat every condition, every time.

2. You **keep asking**, "*And is there anything else that needs to happen for...*" until the client says there are no more conditions to be met.

You can be surprised: All the obvious impediments might be addressed, and you are confident your client has determined all the conditions, but dutifully, you ask one more time... only for your client to discover, for example, an *emotional* impediment, like fear or guilt about leaving others behind.

Alternative example:

Client: *The way over the bridge is blocked, and I can't see clearly what it is!*

Facilitator: And when the way is blocked and you can't see clearly what it is, **what needs to happen for** you to go over that bridge?

Client: *I need to see clearly, to see what it is in the way.*

Facilitator: And you need to see clearly, to see what it is in the way. And **is there anything else that needs to happen for** you to go over that bridge?

Client: *Yes, I may need some help moving that, because now I can see that it's pretty big, and Bridge can't let me through.*

Facilitator: And you need to see clearly, and you may need some help. And **is there anything else that needs to happen for** you to go over Bridge?

Client: *I need to trust Bridge can hold me.*

Facilitator: And you need to see clearly, and you may need some help moving that pretty big... And you need to trust Bridge can hold you. And **is there anything else that needs to happen for** you to go over Bridge?

Client: *I need to know the other side is safe.*

Facilitator: And you need to know the other side is safe. And to trust Bridge will hold you. And you may need some help moving what it is in the way. And see clearly. And **is there anything else that needs to happen for** you to go over Bridge?

Client: *No...no..., that's all.*

Meeting Conditions

Once your client has a complete list of their conditions for change, direct them back through each condition with CLQs. Flesh out the details and check for any other conditions that may be needed to meet the first level of conditions. For example, you might ask of the last client:

> "And what needs to happen for you to see clearly?"
>
> "And what kind of help is that help you may need?"
>
> "And where could that help you may need come from?"
>
> "And what needs to happen for you to get the help you may need?"

In this way, the client will develop a comprehensive list of all the conditions that need to be met, based on the logic of their landscape.

A House of Cards

If the list of conditions is extensive, don't worry! You may not need to address them all with CLQs and Symbolic Modeling. Oftentimes, once your client resolves a few of the conditions, the rest easily seem to resolve themselves, like a tumbling house of cards. It may not be obvious which are the key cards, but you will know when you have found them! With the right ones removed, all the blocks to the change the client initially wanted are suddenly cleared or no longer seem relevant to them. So, rest assured that if you get a long list of conditions from a client, it rarely proves to be as lengthy a process as it may seem at first.

Symbols May Have Conditions for Change, Too

When you ask symbols what they would like to have happen, you may find still other conditions that need to be met before the client's desired changes can occur. These must be added to your client's conditions for change, as they, too, are part of their system.

Example continued:

Facilitator: And you'd like to go over Bridge. And when you'd like to go over Bridge, what would Bridge like to have happen?

Client: *Oh, Bridge isn't sure he likes that idea!! Bridge wants to be sure he won't be lonely.*

Facilitator: And Bridge wants to be sure he won't be lonely. And what needs to happen for Bridge to be sure he won't be lonely?

Client: *He wants me to promise I'll come back to visit.*

Facilitator: And promise you'll come back to visit. And is there anything else Bridge needs to happen for him to be sure he won't be lonely?

Client: *He needs to be sure I'll keep my promise.*

Facilitator: And Bridge needs you to promise to come back to visit, and Bridge needs to be sure you'll keep your promise. And is there anything else that needs to happen for Bridge to be sure he won't be lonely?

Client: *No, that's all.*

Facilitator: And when Bridge wants you to promise to come back to visit, and needs to be sure you'll keep your promise, what needs to happen for Bridge to be sure you'll keep your promise?

Client: *He needs to trust me.*

Facilitator: And he needs to trust you. And be sure you'll keep your promise. And come back to visit. And is there anything else that needs to happen for Bridge to be sure you'll keep your promise?"

Client: *No, that's all.*

And so it goes. You can see how the list of conditions for change of multiple symbols, along with your client's conditions, can really multiply! In essence, each one of them becomes a new sub-desired outcome, all serving the initial desired outcome.

Although facilitating all these many parts may seem overwhelming when you are learning, once you have mastered the basics, this is actually the sort of challenge I suspect you may enjoy. This fantastic puzzle is unfolding before you, and you are helping your client find all the pieces and figure out how they go together and what they want to change. What fun!

4.1 *Activity*

When a client identifies a desired outcome, you don't usually jump right to asking for Conditions for Change, unless the landscape is well-developed, with information about the word and symbols already established. For each of the following client statements, consider what the client might gather more information about that would help them to be able to identify how their system works, and thus, reveal what needs to be done or changed. Ask **at least three CLQ**s to develop that info. Then ask for **conditions for change.**

Example:

Client: I *want to step into a brighter future that I determine for myself.*

Facilitator: And step into a brighter future you determine for yourself...

1) And when determine for yourself, what kind of determine is that determine?
2) And when step into a brighter future, that's step into like what?
3) And when a brighter future, whereabouts is that brighter future?

   Then...

4) And what needs to happen for you to step into that brighter future?

1. The real me wants to come out and really shine!

2. The filter needs to be clear so the water can flow, and the pump can keep pumping.

3. There's a hosta plant in my head and, when it reaches full size, my temple can open, and I will be free.

4. I want us to be intimately connected, like we were when we first started dating.

5. I want to be moving in the same direction as my business partner.

Note-taking

By now you have had a good deal of practice taking notes, so no doubt you are developing a system for yourself. When your client starts to get numerous conditions for change, you may become truly challenged to keep track of what might be a lot of information. I suggest you take some time to think about how you will record a *list of conditions*. You will want to be able to easily keep the whole in mind as you navigate amongst the items on the list. Or maybe you prefer to create a mind map, with the desired outcome in the center.

Personally, as soon as I ask, "And what needs to happen...," I'm ready to start a numbered list on the left side of my page so I have plenty of room to write detailed answers and still be able to locate the list easily when I need it. Here's an example of what my notes might look like:

Example:

Client: *I want to leave this place of easy comfort, and go out into the world.*

Let's assume I have facilitated my client with CLQs so they have developed information about their *place of easy comfort* and the *world they want to go out into*. And let us say they have confirmed again, they want to make this change.

Notice my client has specified two desired outcomes, to *leave this place* and to go *out into the world*. It is surely no accident that they have identified these as two steps; they may have different conditions for the two. Remember to be attentive to increments of time and sequence: the two steps should be explored separately, not lumped together. Let's explore the first condition for change in detail.

Facilitator: And leave this place and go out into the world. And when leave this place of easy comfort, what needs to happen for you to leave this place?

My notes

Conditions:

1. Remind myself all healthy birds outgrow their nest eventually.
2. Close the windows.
3. Lock the door and pocket the key…

   -so I can come back if I want to.

1. Thank Treehouse for taking good care of me.

I kept asking, "And is there anything else that needs to happen for you to leave this place?" until my client has no more conditions.

Example continued:

Facilitator: And [review her list]. And is there *anything else* that needs to happen for you to leave this place of easy comfort?

Client: *No. I could be comfortable and easy about leaving then, and I'd be ready to go!*

Confirmation

It is time to check to see if there are issues with any items on the list by asking the other Conditions for Change question, **CLQ #11**. I am asking *when I am pretty confident the answer is going to be yes*, inviting my client to confirm their readiness and verbalize their resolve aloud.

> **"And can** [D.O.]**?"**

Example continued:

Facilitator: And **can you** remind yourself healthy birds outgrow their nest eventually?

Client: *Yes, it's time.*

Facilitator: And **can you** close the windows?

Client: *Yes, they're closed.*

Facilitator: And **can you** lock the door?

Client: *I can.*

Facilitator: And **can you** pocket that key?

Client: *Yes. It's in my right hip pocket.*

Facilitator: And **can you** come back if you want to?

Client: (tearing up) *This is really important. Now I know I can... I can come back.*

Facilitator: And **can you** thank Treehouse for taking good care of you?

Client: *I've hung a beautiful wreath I made on the door. It's a special thank you. Oh, and I gave Treehouse a special hug.*

Facilitator: And **is there *anything else* that needs to happen** for you to leave this place?

Client: *No, I'm ready.*

Facilitator: And you're ready. And **can you** leave this place of easy comfort?

Client: *Yes! In fact, I already have.*

You see why you will want to make it easy to locate your client's list of conditions in your notes. You will need to tick off the items to be sure you have covered everything.

Now it is time to check on the client's second desired outcome's conditions for change.

Example continued:

Facilitator: And as you leave, comfortable and easy, **can you** go out into the world?

Client: *It's time to leave Treehouse and make my way in the world. I can go.*

Notice the client has slightly changed their wording of their Desired Outcome statement. Don't assume because it is similar that it is the same! Check it out.

Facilitator: And leave Treehouse, and make your way in the world. And is that *make your way in the world* the same as or different than *go out into the world*?

Client: *Now that you ask, I can go out, but I'm not sure about making my way. How will I get food and shelter?*

Oh! New information about the landscape has emerged, a subtle but seemingly significant distinction between *going out* and *making my way* in the world that the client has just noticed. Time to loop back to Stage 2 of the Symbolic Modeling process and start exploring again. There are many ways you could start. How about:

Facilitator: And when making your way in the world, what kind of making is that making, .. when you are making your way in the world?

Ask a few more questions; follow where they lead. Be sure to check to see if the client's desired outcome changes, given new information. For our purposes here, let's assume it is still the same. With more detailed information, you are at Stage 4 again, establishing conditions for change by asking:

Facilitator: And what needs to happen to make your way in the world?

Strategizing

Let's work with another client, this time without invoking a metaphor landscape.

Example:

Client: *I'd like to make good decisions about how I spend my time. I find myself frittering away my time before I settle down to work. Or I get easily distracted and leave things unfinished.*

My strategy: Thinking REPRO, I would start by identifying for myself:

1. Desired Outcome: *to make good decisions about how I spend my time*
2. Problem: *frittering away my time*
3. Resourceful state the client can achieve: *settle down*
4. Problem: *easily distracted*
5. Problem: *leave things unfinished*

My overall plan is to help my client identify their desired outcomes for problems 2, 4, and 5. This will likely affect and/or increase their desired outcomes. But for learning's sake, let us assume that, after all that exploration, my client is clearer than ever that what they want is to address their initial desired outcome: to *make good decisions about how they spend their time*. I want to assist them in better understanding themselves and their patterns.

Brainstorming Possible CLQs

Strategically, I start off asking myself, "What is it my client most likely needs to collect information about?" With this in mind, I suspect this client might benefit from being more aware of:

- And what needs to happen for you to make good decisions?
- And what needs to happen for you to make good decisions about how you spend your time?
- And what happens just before you fritter away your time?
- And what happens just before you settle down to work?
- And is there anything else that needs to happen for you to settle down to work?
- And what happens just before you leave things unfinished?

Like a Game of Chess

I think of a session as playing a game of chess. I plan ahead a few strategic moves, ready to change my questions in response to my client's answers. *It is important not to get so caught up in your plan that you aren't listening and responding to what is happening, just as it would be folly not to notice your chess partner's moves!*

Where to Begin?

So, with all these choices, where would I start with this distractable client? I see "settling down" as a resource state. I would like to help this client identify their sequence of steps for settling down. Ditto for good decision-making: What steps are they aware of? Since I suspect that being settled down will be a prerequisite for making decisions, both logically and because they mention it in the very next sentence after their first one about good decisions, I would start with this trio of "chess moves" in mind.

> "**And what kind of** settle down **is that** settle down?"
>
> "**And what needs to happen** for you to settle down?"
>
> "**And what happens just before** you settle down?"

4.2 *Activity*

I shared my strategy with you as an example, not to suggest it is the one, right way. Where would you start with this same client and why? Share your strategy with your practice buddy.

Client: *I'd like to make good decisions about how I spend my time. I find myself frittering away my time before I settle down to work. Or I get easily distracted and leave things unfinished.*

One more question to consider: at what point would *you* invite this client to get a metaphor?

> **"And that's** settle down...**like...what?"**

FAQ Frequently Asked Questions

Can I ask, "And can [condition for change]?" before all the conditions for change have been fleshed out?

There are no hard and fast rules. Remember, I said to ask the "Can" question when you are fairly sure the answer will be "Yes." If it seems the condition is likely to be complicated or challenging, I avoid asking, "And can you?" then; I don't want to encourage the possibility that the client will feel discouraged. Instead I stick with, "And what needs to happen...?" which gives the client some agency, until we have all the conditions. If some of the items on the emerging conditions list seem easy, I might ask a quick, "And can you?" before continuing to check for more conditions. If the client can come up with a few affirmative answers, perhaps it will feel empowering. and build momentum.

Example revisited:

Client: *I'd like to make good decisions about how I spend my time.*

Facilitator: And what needs to happen for you to make good decisions?

Client: *To start with, I need to gather all the relevant information.*

Facilitator: And can you gather all the relevant information?

Client: *Yes, that I can do. I've got two assistants I can assign to the task.*

Facilitator: And two assistants can gather the relevant information. And is there anything else that needs to happen for you to make good decisions?

Client: *Well, I need to sort through the info. Some stuff will be more relevant than other stuff.*

Facilitator: And can you determine which stuff is more relevant?

Client: *Ah! There's the problem...or one of them. I get bogged down in deciding.*

Facilitator: And when you get bogged down in deciding, what would you like to have happen?

Client: *I'd like to be decisive, not flounder in the shoals! Bam! Just decide!*

Facilitator: And what needs to happen for you to just decide? Bam!

Checking on the *sorting* revealed a new problem, requiring a new desired outcome, which may have new conditions for change. And so it goes!

What if the client's answer is, "No, I can't"?

Suppose your client is deeply immersed in their metaphor world, and you think it is likely that your client's desired change can happen. If you ask, "And can [D.O.]?" and the client answers, "No," the *most likely* reasons are:

a. There are one or more additional unmet condition(s) for change

b. The client doesn't have enough information yet

(There are more complicated reasons that change might not be able to happen, such as when a client has a bind, but we are not going to address them in this Basics course.)

Unmet Condition

You can respond to your client's "No, I can't." by asking for another condition for change:

Facilitator: **And when you can't** [condition for change], **what needs to happen for you to** [condition for change]?

Example:

Facilitator: And to be your True self, you need to speak your mind. And when you can't, what needs to happen for you to speak your mind?

Or, if you're thinking P/R/O, it may occur to you that "No, I can't." is a problem statement. Good for you for noticing! You could ask the problem CLQ:

Facilitator: **And when you can't** [condition for change], **what would you like to have happen?**

Example:

Facilitator: And you need to speak your mind. And when you can't speak your mind, what would you like to have happen?

More Information Needed

Sometimes just asking more *Anything else, What kind of,* and other developing questions will help the client gather the information they need.

There may be another symbol in the landscape with a desired outcome that conflicts with your client's, as we discussed in Section Two. A new condition for change might be for the client and the symbol to come to some sort of understanding. Be curious!

Getting a Running Start

Sometimes all seems to be in readiness, and still a client hesitates on the brink of change. If you have checked repeatedly, and the client keeps repeating that nothing else needs to happen, but the change doesn't happen, there is something else going on.

Any number of things could be happening, some of which we have discussed, but as you have been learning the REPROCess model in this basics course, let's consider one way to approach this situation: focus on your client's resources. You can try reviewing all that is ready, heightening your client's embodied sense of their own resources and their encouraging self-talk. This can help build up some momentum, like getting a running start that propels them.

Here is an example where I am using **time questions** along with **condition for change questions** to help my client take the next step they have said they are eager to take.

Example:

Client: *I know I can cross this bridge, but I'm hesitating.*

Facilitator: And you know you can cross. And when you know you can cross, and you're hesitating, **what needs to happen for** you to cross that bridge?

Client: *I'm not sure. It's something about knowing I can.*

Facilitator: And you know you can cross that bridge. And when you know you can, **what happens just before** you know you can?

Client: *I remind myself I've done it before.*

Facilitator: And you've done it before. And is there **anything else that happens just before** you know you can?

Client: *I tell myself, "If I can do it once, I can do it again!"*

Facilitator: And you remind yourself, "I've done it before." And you tell yourself, "If I can do it once, I can do it again." And **then what happens?**

Client: *Then I'm not scared anymore, and I can cross!*

Facilitator: And you're not scared any more. And you can cross! And is there a**nything else that needs to happen** after you're not scared anymore and **before** you can cross?

Client: *No. Huh! I feel older now. More mature. Stronger.*

Facilitator: And older, more mature, stronger. And when you are older, more mature, and stronger, is there **anything else that needs to happen for** you to cross?

Client: *Wow! I really can do it! I'm crossing: I'm just walking calmly. I feel confident and assured. What was I so worried about? The hesitating is just gone.*

Notice in the example above how the client doesn't always directly answer my question. That happens! You have to be really listening, adjust, and incorporate whatever your client comes up with! You read how I used time questions to discover and expand on the conditions and inner resources my client needed in order to cross. In an actual session, I would take even more time to develop these resources (like mature, stronger,...assured), and the client's embodied experience of them. But remember: the client will be ready when they are ready, and not before! Be sure you are following your client's lead and desires.

"The Boat Trip" Transcript

The following abridged transcript will give you an idea of how an actual session often unfolds, for clients don't tend to discover information in neat, linear or chronological order. With the actual client, I would develop the desired outcome and resources more, as often that can be enough for the needed change to happen. It can turn out that the client doesn't need to resolve each of the problems; they fade away when the desired outcome is clarified. But not always. So, let's assume this is one of those times when the client needs to learn more about other conditions for change they want. (This example is to demonstrate this process, and does not include all the repeating I would do for an actual client.)

1. Client: *I'm in a boat on a silver lake, and the engine is stalled. I can see the island in the distance ahead of me.*

2. Facilitator: And when you're in that boat, and engine is stalled, what would you like to have happen?

3. Client: *I want to get the engine going so I can get out to the island. If I can get to that island, I know I will find peace and regain my true sense of self. But I'm not mechanical! I can't fix this thing!*

4. Facilitator: And what needs to happen to get that engine going, when you are not mechanical, and you can't fix this thing?

5. Client: *I need help fixing the engine, but there's no one in sight to help.*

6. Facilitator: And what needs to happen for help to fix the engine, when there's no one in sight?

7. Client: *I guess I wait. Sometimes you just have to have patience, and wait awhile for what you need.*

8. Facilitator: And as you wait, is there anything else that needs to happen to get to the island, where you will find peace… and true sense of self?

9. Client: *I'm worried there may be sandbars or rocks I can't see just under the surface. The boat might go down if it hits something.*

10. Facilitator: And sandbars and rocks… just under the surface. And when all that, what would you like to have happen?

11. Client: *I'd be a lot more at ease if I knew the boat could cross the water safely! I wish I could quit this fretting; it's exhausting. This is supposed to be a pleasurable outing, but this is stressful!*

12. Facilitator: And what needs to happen for you to know the boat could cross safely?

13. Client: *If I had sonar, I could locate underwater obstacles. I want to know in advance of anything I'm approaching that the boat could strike.*

14. Facilitator: And sonar. And patience. And help to fix the engine. And is there anything else that needs to happen for you to get to that island?

15. Client: *Now there's fog rolling in.*

16. Facilitator: And fog rolling in. And what kind of fog is that fog that's rolling in?

17. Client: *It's oddly thick, not misty. I can't see the island anymore. I need to see the island to set my course. I need to find a way to get this fog to part and let me through.*

18. Facilitator: And you need to set your course. And find a way to get Fog to part and let you through. And when get Fog to part and let you through, what would Fog like to have happen?

19. Client: *Fog is not keen on letting me through. He doesn't think I'm ready to get to the island.*

20. Facilitator: And are you ready to get to that island... and find peace... and true self ?

21. Client: *Yes, I am. I know I am.*

22. Facilitator: And how do you know you are ready?

23. Client: *I know because of the way I feel when I see the island. It's a knowing in my solar plexus that it's where I belong. It's home.*

24. Facilitator: And what needs to happen for Fog to let you through?

25. Client: *He needs to have faith in me. (...continues)*

Keep developing this session in your imagination. Imagine what Fog responds to this new information, what you would ask next, and so on. People often ask me how I mastered Clean Language, and I can tell you, this is the sort of game I would play in my head. The advantage over practicing with a real client (which, of course, has its benefits!) is that you can take all the time you need to figure out what you are going to ask, you can easily change your mind and ask another question, and you can make the client's answers as easy or complex as you like. You can always practice at exactly your comfort level.

4.3 *Activity*

Take your time to deconstruct the client's statements in The Boat Trip. Identify the following in the margins of the transcript:

- Client's **D**esired **O**utcomes
- **P**roblems and **R**emedies
- **C**onditions for **C**hange—to achieve the Desired Outcome
- **Res**ources

Compare your list to your practice buddy's. What do you notice?

4.4 *Activity*

Review your list of the client's conditions for change on your Boat Trip transcript. As you have no real client to work with, practice by applying common sense to determine the most logical sequence in which those conditions would need to be met (ex. usually a motor has to be fixed before it can move a boat). **Note the order in the margin** by numbering the conditions for change in sequence. Compare this with a practice partner's ordering. Have you made different assumptions?

This exercise is to get you thinking about a landscape's *inherent logic* and *noticing sequence*. It will help you experience how clients' information sometimes emerges non-sequentially. Once your client gets to "nothing more needs to happen", thinking about the logic of the landscape may help you decide of which condition to first ask, "And can you [x]?" or "And what needs to happen to/for…?"

A *Clean* Alternative

In an actual session, you have the option of asking your client in what order they think conditions need to be addressed. What could be cleaner? What they attend to will inform you both about their patterns, priorities, and the logic of their internal world. You could create a specialized question along the lines of:

> **"And when** [list conditions], **what needs to happen first?"**

> **"And what needs to happen next?"**

Repeat until all the conditions are addressed or until the "house of cards falls" and, suddenly, everything is different. What do I mean? To use The Boat Trip example, perhaps once the motor is running, presto! The client might suddenly be on the island and focused on getting to know a whole new part of their landscape. If that happens, conditions for dealing with the fog and the sonar may no longer be relevant. When we get to Stage 5, you will see how you can help your client find out if they are still problematic.

Tracking with Post-it notes

I have become a huge fan of having clients write down their Desired Outcome(s) and Conditions for Change on Post-it notes to track these important elements of their landscape. It's a sort of hybrid verbal/enacting-the-metaphor session. The beauty of Post-its is that they are easy to move around as new information emerges. And that's a great benefit because *where* the client places their words in relation to other words (how far from, above, below, in what order, etc.) often signifies significant information.

Another benefit is, as when working with drawings, Post-it notes relieve you of much note-taking. In a session where the list of conditions is long and where those conditions have their own conditions, there can be a considerable amount of information for you and for the client to keep track of. So, let the client do the work! It's okay to get conversational for a moment, suggest your client get a pen and Post-its (for in-person sessions, I always have some on hand), map out what they know so far, and then resume your CLQs. You will want to use these two specialized CLQs and directives for when your client mentions something new.

> **"And put that down."**

> **"And where could that (**referring to a new Post-it) **be/go?"**

The client can stick the Post-its on a blank wall, a door, a white board, or lay them on a desktop or the floor-- any clear space where they can view them as a whole. Something happens when they stand back and see what they wrote. Be prepared for them to stare a lot and take long pauses as they process what emerges. Most will look at you when they are ready for another question.

4.5 *Activity*

If you recognize these next statements, it is because you have seen these before in the workbook, *Basics Part One*. I thought you might enjoy revisiting them with new eyes. Think now in terms of identifying what change the client desires, their desired outcomes, and practicing asking for conditions for change by saying it aloud. To extend this activity, you can do a lot of strategizing with the statements below as to what else you might ask.

1. I get so serious and task-driven. My wife says I'm a workaholic, and I do get tension headaches. She says I need to take it easy more, but I can't sit around and do nothing! I like to be active; if only I could do that in a more relaxed way—more playful, maybe.

2. Lately, I've been really testy around the office. Maybe it's the economy. I worry that every little criticism is a hint that the axe might fall! I'd like to feel more flexible about how I respond to situations. I just get defensive so quickly—like a knee-jerk reaction. Whatever happens, that's not helping matters!

3. I'm highly critical of myself. What I do is never good enough. I wish I could be more accepting and compassionate with myself. I read a self-help book on this; can you recall the author's name? A really well-known celebrity... you know who I mean?

4. I'd like to not allow my emotions to rule my actions or determine my mood. I'd like to be able to motivate myself. I'd like to find healthy ways to get out of difficult situations, not use food or TV/avoidness to cope with uncomfortable situations or emotions. I'm trying to eat more vegetables, but they're just not very compelling! (Note: If your client uses a grammatically incorrect word like avoidness, you should repeat it exactly unless they correct it.)

5. I've found myself lately in a place where I'm really anxious when I'm talking to my husband when it's just the two of us. I'd like to feel I can stay calm and talk openly and honestly with him.

Answers in the back.

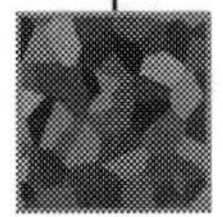

"Real Life" Applications

We have been talking mostly about applying "conditions for change" modeling to metaphor landscapes. But when it comes to exploring choices and making plans for action in the everyday world, you can use these same Clean Language questions and modeling strategies.

Examples:

- Determining what needs to happen, where, and when for your client to practice visualizing their resource metaphor for relaxation
- Developing a business plan
- Mapping a strategy for a difficult conversation with a family member
- Going about getting a new job
- Helping a parent come up with a strategy for their child's homework time

4.6 *Activity*

Time to practice with a partner. For about 20 minutes, focus on identifying a desired change and a list of conditions. The chart on the next page is here to assist you, with some less-often used developing questions and room for you to add a Specialized question or two you would like to practice. I suggest using Post-its; it will make you job easier, facilitators!

The partner being the client is welcome to go into fantasy here: Come up with a desired change right off the bat, make up a list of 3–5 conditions, have 1 or 2 of them have a condition to be met, but keep each one short. In other words, clients should give their facilitators information to work with, without being overwhelming.

Afterward, answer the following:

Something I did well was:

Something I want to work on next time is:

CHART: Conditions for Change

CONDITIONS FOR CHANGE

1. Identify Desired Outcome using P/R/O

    And what would you like to have happen?

    And when [remedy reworded]**, then what happens?**

2. Gather information with Developing and Specialized CLQs

    Some options:

    And **where** could that [x] **come from**?

    And what happens **just before** [x]?

    And is there a **relationship between** that [x] and that [y]?

    And **what do you know** about that [x]?

    And **how much more** [x] do you want?

    And when many [x's], **how many** could there be?

    ____

    ____

3. Gather a list of Conditions for Change for each Desired Outcome

    And **what needs to happen for** [x]?

    And is there **anything else** that **has to happen for** [x]?

4. Check that each Condition for Change and Desired Outcome can be met

    And **can** [x]?

Section Four Summary

Your client identifies when they are **ready for change** and what they want to have happen. Your job is not to fix things for your client or push them along.

Use Clean Language questions to explore all that needs to happen for your client to achieve their desired outcomes. These are their **conditions for change**.

Just as symbols can have **desired outcomes**, they can also have **conditions for change**.

Use time questions, revisit resources, and ask conditions for change questions to **build momentum** before your client s to make a change.

Establishing conditions for change is a modeling strategy that can be applied to everyday life issues as well as metaphor landscapes.

My take-away from this section is...

Questions I have...

4.7 Review Activity

Unfortunately, clients don't tend to give you information in single sentences. Nor do problems, remedies, and outcomes come neatly bundled in a straightforward, linear fashion. Here are some lengthier passages to work with. If you have a practice partner, they can read the statement aloud and take on the role of the client, making up information as you go.

Directions: Think **REPROC**ess!

Listen for **E**xplanations that you want to avoid putting attention on.

Think **P/R/O** and **R**esources to help you determine what you ask for more information about.

Be sure the client has a clear **D**esired **O**utcome.

Get **C**onditions for **C**hange for desired outcome(s). (Hint: Some of the conditions may already be stated. Identify them, and include them in your repetitions!)

1. I get these tension headaches near the end of the day, and they make me really cranky. I'm just not efficient at that point, and I think my partner's irritated. If only we could have more of a meeting of the minds, so to speak. His peak time, the height of his energy, is around 4 p.m. We're just really mismatched that way.

2. I've started working remotely full-time now, and I'm having a really hard time, much more than I thought I would. I feel so isolated, and I really miss the camaraderie. I even miss the people who used to drive me crazy! Like this guy, Luke. He used to whistle all the time. Drove me nuts!! It's those around-the-coffee pot moments I really miss, the casual conversations that can't happen at an online meeting. It's really got me down.

3. I've always aspired to be really good at something, and I have lots of interests, have tried lots of things, but I seem to run out of steam before too long and move on to something else. Like my cousin is really good at chess; he plays against people on the Internet. I tried that for a while, too, but I gave it up. I just want to know, deep inside, that I'm good enough to really be great at something!

4. I can be doing ordinary chores, you know, like washing the dishes or taking out the garbage, and suddenly, I'm flooded with memories of my late wife. Sometimes that's really nice, and other times it brings me to my knees. Seems like she was always in the kitchen doing something, you know? Man, could she cook! Everyone in the family loved her pies.

5. I am a single parent, and it's really hard. There's just never a down-time, never a time I'm off duty. My kids are teenagers now, so they're up later than I am! It's not like when they were little, and I would put them to bed and have an hour or two to myself. I miss that! We have a small house; they do their homework at the kitchen table, and that closeness is nice, or I guess it could be, but it's stressful, too. It's like riding in a crowded subway; we're all in each others' space, bumping elbows and reading the book the guy next to you is holding, over his shoulder.

Answers in the back.

Section Five

"What I thought was an end turned out to be a middle.
What I thought was a brick wall turned out to be a tunnel.
What I thought was injustice turned out to be a color of the sky."

--Tony Hoagland

Maturing the Landscape

You are now ready for Stage 5 of the Symbolic Modeling process. Once your client's conditions for change have been met and a change occurs in the landscape, you will want to help your client explore its effects on themselves, their other symbols, the symbols' relationships, and previously stated problems and desired outcomes. We call it *maturing* the landscape.

Metaphorically speaking, you help a change ripen and bear fruit.

You may recall this graphic representation of your client's internal system from *Basics Part One*. It shows your client's network of interconnected relationships. Change a metaphor, and all connected parts (of which just a few are shown in the diagram) can be affected because they are *in relationship.*

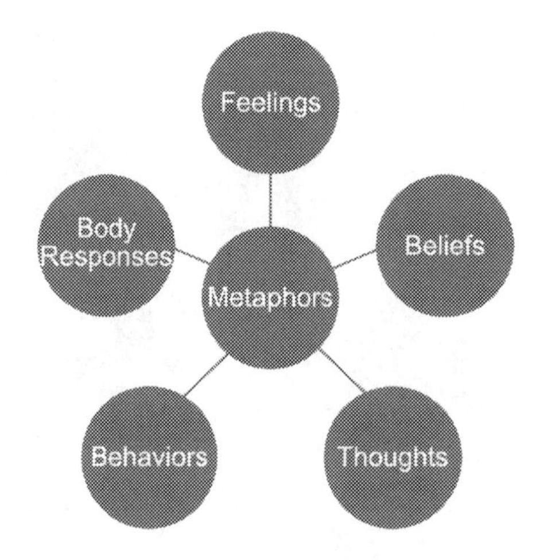

To describe it another way, people are self-organizing systems: when new information is introduced (such as a change), all parts of their systems will rearrange as needed to accommodate that information. The system learns from itself.

Effects of Maturing

- Develops all aspects of the change
- Encourages all parts of the system to respond to the change with their own adjustments
- Helps your client embody the change, noticing how and where they feel its effects
- Reveals any problems that still need resolving
- Sustains the change
- Makes relapse less likely

If the change is a significant one, maturing can help:

- An old pattern fade and a new pattern become the go-to response
- The client become familiar with and practice a new way of being

Persistent attention to maturing changes in the landscape can yield big rewards. Even small changes can snowball until your client's entire landscape reorganizes. Old symbols or patterns may morph or disappear. Your client can experience a *transformed* inner world!

Checking in with Other Aspects of the Landscape

When you mature a change, you are guiding your client to pay attention to a larger part of the whole landscape. To recall our camera analogy from Section Three, you are *zooming* out. You want to help your client notice:

1. **What is new in the moment**
2. **What happens to their previously existing landscape**
3. **What happens moving forward, after the change**

As a facilitator, you want to maintain a good balance between these three foci as you direct your client's attention so they can find out what's new and what differences the new changes are making. The more time spent familiarizing them with the changes, the more comfortable they will be with them, and the more likely their system will not reject them.

I think of it like a new hairstyle: sometimes I feel awkward and a bit uncomfortable at first, even if I like it. It takes awhile for me to settle into it, until I feel like me with it. The difference is, with a new hairstyle, if it involves a substantive change—if my hair was cut, say—there is no going back, at least not anytime soon; I am forced to live with it. But in your client's landscape, a relapse is, theoretically, always possible; the old pattern and neural pathways are still there. You want to firmly establish the new neural pathways. You can do this by helping your client feel at home in their new landscape with their "new self." Spending time maturing the landscape will do that.

1. New in the Moment

Further develop the new information your client gets by using your basic **CL** and **specialized questions**, such as:

> "**And when** [x changes], …
>
> > **is there anything else about** [changed x]?"
> >
> > **what kind of** [changed x] **is that** [changed x]?"
> >
> > **whereabouts is** [changed x]?"

2. Existing Landscape

There are a number of questions you can use to inquire about other aspects of the landscape to examine the effect(s) of a change. This CLQ, the last of SyM's 12 basic questions, is categorized as a **relationship** question:

Clean Language Question #12: Maturing Change

CLQ: And when [x changes], **what happens to** [previous y]?

You can check back in on problems, on symbols, on resources, but the most significant things to check back on are any *desired outcomes* that emerged in the session. Are they achievable now? If one is not, you will need to go back to Stage 4 and ask, "*And what/what else needs to happen...*?" Generally, we go back through the D.O.s in reverse order, but follow the logic of the landscape more than this rule of thumb. You can see why, in *Basics Part One*, I recommended you marked D.O.s in your notes; having an easy way to spot them makes this part of maturing much easier!

3. Moving Forward

Once a change takes place, use the same **advancing time questions** that you have already learned. It is just that, now, you can be thinking about their purpose differently. When the client advances the landscape forward in time after a change, it helps concretize it.

And when/as [x changes],

...what happens next?

...then what happens?

To demonstrate, let's go back to the example with the client who wants to cross the bridge (Section Four), and assume the client and Bridge have worked out their conflicting Desired Outcomes. Using the six questions useful for maturing above, I will direct the client's attention to mature their landscape.

Example:

Client: *I can feel now, under my feet, that Bridge is strong.*

Facilitator: And under your feet, Bridge is strong. And when Bridge is strong, **what happens to** strong enough?

Client *Bridge is strong enough to hold me.*

Facilitator: And Bridge is strong enough to hold you. And when strong enough, **what happens to** trust?

Client: *I can trust it now. I'm going to be safe going across.*

Facilitator: And you can trust it now. And you're going to be safe going across. **And is there anything else about** that safe?

Client: *It's a safe I can count on, that Bridge will stay solid under my feet.*

Facilitator: And when safe you can count on and solid under your feet, **what happens to** blocked?

Client: *The blocks are gone! They're simply gone, and I can see the other side clearly now.*

Facilitator: And you can see the other side clearly. And you can feel Bridge strong and solid under your feet. And **what kind of** feet are those feet, when you can feel Bridge?

Client: *They're strong, too! They can take me across. Huh! That's what I really needed, was to be strong enough myself to get across!!*

Facilitator: And strong enough yourself! And blocks are gone, and you can see the other side clearly. And when you can see the other side clearly, **whereabouts is** that other side?

Client: *It's only six feet or so in front of me now. I'm almost there. It looks so inviting. I can hardly wait to get there!*

Facilitator: And you're strong enough to get yourself across, and feet are strong, and Bridge is strong and solid, and you can trust it. You can see the other side clearly, and it's only six feet in front of you, and it's so inviting. And when all that, **what happens next?**

This example demonstrates just *some* of the questions you could ask to mature the change, connecting to previous symbols and desired outcomes and finding out more about this new state of being, all in preparation for the client's actual step to the other side...when they are ready. Your thoroughness helps assure your client has no unfinished business, no remaining unresolved problems, that could undermine lasting change.

Embody the Change

Notice, too, how my repetitions and questions have encouraged this client to *embody* their new state by focusing their attention on some of their body's resources: their feet, their strength. What about their statement: "I can hardly wait to get there!"? Their eagerness could be a resource, too (although they haven't named it yet!). What about their newfound *trust* of the bridge?

You see how you could easily spend considerable time here, at this moment of change.

Variation on the Maturing Question

Just as with the middle phrase of the full syntax wording, "And when [x],...," you have a choice with the basic maturing question to replace when with as.

CLQ: "And *as* [x], what happens to [y]?"

If it is easier for you as a beginner learning all these new questions to just keep using *when*, it will still work fine. But as you get more comfortable with the nuances of your word choices and what is going on for your client, you can add this subtle refinement. You may recall from earlier (Section One) that you replace *when* with *as* when the client is actually *experiencing the change in the moment*. In the previous example, that would sound like:

Example:

Facilitator:	And strong enough to get yourself across, And feet are strong, and Bridge is strong and solid. You can see the other side clearly, and it's only six feet in front of you, and it's so inviting. And when all that, **what happens next?**
Client:	*I'm going across now.*
Facilitator:	And going across now. And **as** you're going across, **what happens to** feet?
Client:	*They feel determined and confident.*

Notice how I am slowing down my client with lots of repetition, encouraging them to check in to see if anything else is happening now, encouraging them to notice their feet and relish their embodied state. Don't be in a hurry to "get your client to the other side," curious as you may be to see what happens next.

Maturing and New Metaphors

As you mature the shifts in your client's landscape, it is not unusual for new metaphors to appear. In this example, the client discovers a resourceful new way of being/feeling. I will take time to develop it and help the client know it better. The more comfortable and excited they are with the new way of being, the less apt they are to want to go back to the old way of being.

Example continued:

Facilitator:	And going across. And determined and confident feet. And when confident, **is there anything else about that confident, when feet feel confident?**
Client:	*I'm at the other side now. Aha! I made it... This is weird. My feet are turning into bird's feet.*
Facilitator:	And turning into bird's feet. And **is there anything else** about those bird's feet?
Client:	*I'm free like a bird, no longer tethered to the earth. Free to fly when and where I will.*
Facilitator:	And a bird, and free to fly when and where you will. And when free like a bird, **what kind of** bird is that bird?
Client:	*A strong bird. Not big, but looks are deceptive. This is a bird who can migrate thousands of miles if he wants to.*

Facilitator: And **as** your feet are turning into bird's feet, **then what happens?**

Client: *I am that strong bird. I can fly.*

Other times, the new metaphor does not present itself. But you may notice the client describes a new resourceful feeling/state. Invite them to discover the metaphor:

Variation on example:

Facilitator: And determined and confident feet. And going across. And when confident, **is there anything else** about that confident, when feet feel confident?

Client: *I'm at the other side now. I have this sense of new-found freedom!*

Facilitator: And a sense of new-found freedom. And when sense of freedom, **that's** freedom **like what?**

Client: *I feel free like a bird, no longer tethered to the earth. Free to fly when and where I will.*

You will notice the client did not seem to address the first question. Okay—that is the client's choice to make. The facilitator followed the client's attention rather than repeat the question, and there was an internalized metaphor!

A Changed Self

Not only should you gather information about new symbols, but also consider that the client themselves may be "new," that is, different in some significant way. You can explore this new self as you would any new symbols. Here is one way to start that *cleanly*:

Example:

Client: *I walked through the gate, and I step out into the sunshine.*

Facilitator: And you step out into the sunshine. And is there anything else about that sunshine?

Client: *It warms and gives life to everything it touches.*

Facilitator: And it gives life and warms. And you step out into that sunshine. And as you step out into that sunshine, **what kind of** *you* **is that** *you*, that steps out into that sunshine that warms and gives life to everything it touches?

Maturing with a metaphor map

Yet another way to mature a landscape is to have the client draw a metaphor map. Personally, I always invite my clients to draw one after a session. It physicalizes what, in most instances, they have been mentally visualizing. It gives them something to keep that can serve as a reminder of the session.

And, to our point here, the experience of drawing gives clients another opportunity to mature their landscape, to discover what it looks like now, after a change(s). It's not unusual for a client to draw something at this time that did not come up during the session. As their mind/ body system restructures, even a few minutes can be time enough for more rippling effects to filter throughout.

Finally, consider that inviting your client to draw removes you and your choices of where to direct attention from your client's the maturing process. You are entrusting the client with the opportunity to discover what needs discovering in the moment.

Specialized Maturing Questions

Recall this specialized question from David Grove's Clean Space technique (*see Basics Part One*, Section Four). You can mature a change by asking:

> **"And what difference does that knowing** [x/all that] **make?"**

Example:

Client: *When I step into the sunshine, I know I can speak my truth.*

Facilitator: And step into the sunshine and you know you can speak your truth. And when you know you can speak your truth, **what difference does knowing that make?**

As asking about a difference is a more cognitive-sounding question that tends to invite analysis and/or the application of a new whole to what happens outside of the session, I usually ask this question at the *end* of a session, just as it is used in the Clean Space process.

If your intention is to keep your client in their metaphor landscape, you might still use this question, but be prepared: your client may pop out of their symbolic domain and "go cognitive." If that happens, just follow the SyM process:

Review:

- Acknowledge a bit of this non-symbolic content by repeating it.
- Backtrack to and review information from the metaphor landscape.

Direct Attention:

- Ask another CLQ about the landscape.

Example continued:

Facilitator: And what difference does knowing that make?

Client: *I know I can tell my father I don't want to be in the military. He won't want to hear it! He pushed my brothers into it; they're both in the Navy. I'm not cut out for it like they are. But Dad's always sure he knows what's best for everyone.*

Facilitator: And your father won't want to hear it. And you know you can speak your truth when you step out into the sunshine. And when sunshine, what happens just before you step out into that sunshine?

I hope by this time you would not be tempted to wade into the mire of sorting out what it is about the Navy that is a problem, anything about the client's brothers, or even their relationship with their father. Remember: it's not about the *content*, it is about the client's process. How do they handle a situation, *any situation*, in which their truth and someone else's are at odds? Help empower them to speak their truth when they want to, and they will likely be capable of sorting out the rest for themselves.

Adding *Now* to Your Questions

When a change has occurred, the landscape shifts. Your client's priorities, desired outcomes, perspective, as well as attributes of symbols and so on, may have shifted, too. To enhance your client's awareness of this different landscape, you might add the word "now" to your questions. It is a subtle way of suggesting that new possibilities could exist. Your client may want to update their desired outcome(s); they may notice other changes.

"And when/as [x change]**, what would you like to have happen *now*?"**

Example:

Facilitator: And you open the gate and step into a new world. And as you step into that new world, what would you like to have happen now?

Conditions for Change and Maturing

If you remember back to Section Four when we covered Conditions for Change, I said that one possible strategy is to get a list of all the conditions before going back to explore them one by one. I also mentioned that often you don't end up having to go back through the whole list-- that a change may happen, and its effects will ripple through some or all of the other items in the system. But the client might not be aware of the effects without you drawing their attention to the items again. If you think of Conditions for Change as sub-desired outcomes, that are necessary for some more primary desired outcome, it makes sense that you would mature them. Likely some of the conditions will be met given the change, and some will present new problems and/or further conditions to be met.

5.1 *Activity*

Here are statements with a list of Conditions for Change and a change described. Use this bulleted list such as you might have in your notes, or perhaps they are represented by your client's individual Post-it notes, to practice asking the maturing questions. Play with the scenarios with your imagination, if you like.

And when [change], what happens to [item x]?

And when [change], can you [c for c]?

1. Desired Outcome: be at peace with myself as I am
   C for C:
   - turn down the volume of critical voices in my head
   - be okay with being less than perfect
   - be okay with my past shortcomings
   - set realistic goals for myself

   Change: *I accept myself as I am.*

2. Desired Outcome: get the energy running properly between Head, Heart, and Gut
   C for C:
   - know how many and where the gears are
   - grease them, so turn with ease
   - replace the broken chain that links them
   - turn on the activating switch
   - assure there will always be enough energy
   - awareness keeps energy flowing and gears turning

   Change: *There is a man with a flashlight, in a stained mechanic's overalls, behind my eyes.*

3. Desired Outcome: know I am ready to climb Mount Everest
   C for C:
   - have the right equipment
   - hire an expert Sherpa
   - save enough money
   - attract a sponsor
   - get a team of climbers
   - do some less challenging practice climbs
   - enhance my physical stamina
   - workout routine, get a trainer
   - enhance my mental stamina
   - be reasonably confident I will be safe

   Change: *I have been invited by National Geographic to join an expedition.*

FAQ Frequently Asked Questions

What if my client doesn't wait for me to mature the change?

You may have great plans to do all this maturing in the moment and with the previously mentioned information...and your client doesn't wait for you. (e.g. They go right on over that bridge and into a new landscape!) Or something totally unexpected happens. "The customer is always right"; you don't want to convey a sense that your client has made a mistake. Just skillfully weave in your maturing questions as you review this new step, directing your client's attention to include what happens next, as well as the impact on the already-established landscape this new development has. Once you have developed this information, you can continue to mature the change forward in time (e.g. You help the client explore the other side, past the bridge.)

How does moving my client forward in time after a change help concretize it?

When a client moves forward into a "new" landscape, where the change will have to have occurred in order for the landscape to be the way it is now or for the client to be where they are now, the old way is left behind. The more familiar they are with the new, the more comfortable they get with it, the less likely it is that the client will go back to the old. Remember, however, this does not mean you should rush through! (And then what happens...and then? and then?) Maturing thoroughly by asking lots of CLQs is the key to ensuring no unresolved issues remain to undermine new change. A new building erected on a shaky foundation may not stand for long!

Are some changes more significant than others?

Yes, of course. But neither you nor your client can be sure when changes first occur which ones will prove to be important. The "size" of a change does not necessarily coincide with its ultimate significance in the client's landscape or life. Be comfortable with not knowing, continue exploring, and see how things unfold. A significant change may be obvious and directly related to the questions you ask, or it may come about without your guidance. Sometimes it is signaled by something as subtle as a shift in your client's expression or when they pause in the midst of talking. Other times, the client notices a significant new piece of information about a symbol, or the client or symbol takes some new action. Just be curious, and follow the process. Mature the changes! Only then will you know which ones are significant. Then, or when your client comes back for their next appointment, or even months later.

Will the change stick?

Maybe yes, maybe no. I have had a client tell me that their experience after just one session led to a whole new attitude towards exercising, and what had been a struggle for several years was simply no longer an issue, even several months later. Changes that are more at the identity level generally do not resolve so readily. Your client will change when they are ready to change, when their system has learned what it needs to know about itself, when it reprocesses what needs reprocessing. *Remember: It is not your job to change your client.*

What if my client returns exactly as they were last week?

First of all, it is an assumption on your part that they are the same person they were before they came in for your last session; you can't really know. But if you mean they return reporting that they have noticed no change or that they seem to have relapsed, a number of things may have happened. Consider these possibilities:

- There may still be something in their metaphor landscape preventing the change. Perhaps a symbol or another "part" of the client has yet to be discovered or it has a conflicting intention. Like a magnet, some unresolved problem or fear may have drawn the client back over that change threshold it seemed they had crossed last session, and they are running their familiar pattern again.
- Perhaps some needed resource is not yet strong enough or your client has trouble accessing it when they need it.
- Your client has had some new realization or factored in another aspect of the situation or considered another value that has caused the landscape to revert.
- Lasting change may require not just that blocks are cleared, but that effort and self-discipline are applied. Behavioral change can, but doesn't always, happen with the flick of a metaphoric switch. Your client may have to *practice* the new way of being and acting until it becomes ingrained.
- You are learning only the *basics* of Symbolic Modeling here. Suffice it to say for now that there are more advanced strategies for working with changes that the client finds difficult to make or maintain.

When a client returns for their next session and reports the change did not stick, ask yourself: what has been revealed about your client's *pattern* of being in the world? You could have your client explore what happened *just before* they relapsed. Where do these answers suggest your client might focus their attention in today's session?

Can Symbolic Modeling help my client develop new habits?

New habits generally form by repeating new behavior. *Continued revisiting of a new resourceful state of being and feeling in the symbolic domain, including evoking resource metaphors, is one way of giving your client practice.* Not all parts of the brain distinguish actual events from imagined ones. (Have you ever woken from a nightmare with your heart pounding? Your body's physical response to the fearful situation was not different because it was only a dream!) Experiential processes like Symbolic Modeling that invoke emotions and sensory images engage the brain at a subconscious level and heighten neuroplasticity. Old neural pathways fade and, with repetition, the new ones become the better-established, go-to paths.[3] Consider, too, how efficient such experiential practice is: your client doesn't have to wait for a real-life situation to occur to exercise their new strategy or resource; they can practice in a session and strengthen those "new muscles".

Can I use other techniques to concretize changes in a Symbolic Modeling session?

In a word, yes. Changes your client has processed in a mindful state with SyM can be reinforced at a later time in many other ways. Just be sure you choose the times to do so with sensitivity to your client's altered-state experience. We will consider this further in Section Six.

5.2 *Activity*

Time for a partner practice. If possible, work with a partner with whom you have just completed a session so you will have a landscape to work with that has plenty of information you can go back and mature once a change occurs. Remember, you can mature *any* change. You can't always tell from the *size* of change how significant it will be to the landscape. Allow 30–40 minutes apiece. You can use the chart on the next page to help you remember the change process.

Afterwards, answer the following questions:

Something I did well was:

Something I want to work on next time is:

CHART: Facilitating Change

FACILITATING CHANGE

1. Client identifies and develops a **Desired Outcome.**
   And what would you like to have happen?
   And that's [D.O.] like what?
   And what kind of [D.O. metaphor] is that [D.O. Metaphor]?

2. Establish **Conditions for Change**
   And what needs to happen for [D.O.]?
   And is there anything else that needs to happen for [D.O.]?
   And can [condition happen]?

3. **Maturing the Change** when the change is [changed x]

   In the moment:

   And is there anything else about [changed x]?
   And what kind of [changed x] is that [changed x]?
   And whereabouts is [changed x] now?

   Other basic CLQs and specialized questions

   What came before:

   And when/as [changed x], what happens to [y]?
   And when/as [changed x], is there anything else about that [y]?

   After the change:

   And when [changed x], then what happens?

   New Metaphor:

   And that's [changed x] like what?

   Specialized question:

   And what difference does knowing [changed x/all that] make?

   New intention:

   And what would you like to have happen now?

Section Five Summary

When a metaphor changes, all connected parts, including other metaphors, can be affected because they are in **relationship**.

Maturing the landscape means you explore how a change affects symbols and relationships in the landscape and all stated desired outcomes, Maturing involves:

- **Developing new information** in the present about the new change
- **Checking existing symbols** and **desired outcomes** to see how these aspects of the landscape have responded
- **Moving the client forward** in time to help concretize the change

A new self. A change can mean the client is different in significant ways. Explore that new "I" the same way you would another symbol.

My take-away from this section is...

Questions I have...

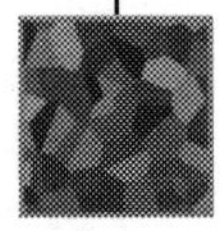

5.3 *Review Activity*

For each of the following statements, first identify any change(s). Then, plan at least three CLQs to...

1) **Develop new information about the change or the changed landscape**

Ex. And is there anything else about [new x]?

And that's [new x] like...what?

2) **Check for changes in the previously-existing landscape**

Ex. And when [new x], what happens to [previous y]?

3) **Move forward in time**

Ex. A when [new x], then what happens?

1. I've always dreaded visiting my brother. You just knew it was going to be miserable, like going to have a tooth drilled! So, I went last weekend, and his partner went at it again, criticizing my kids, personal comments about their clothes, their hair, their coordination, the music they like. Belittling comments. But this time, I said, "Enough." I stood up for my kids, and when he tried to laugh it off, I told the kids, "We're leaving." And we did!

2. I have had a terrible time with insomnia over the last 3 months. Sometimes, I had trouble falling asleep. Sometimes, I could fall asleep, but I had trouble staying asleep. Since I've been envisioning that pond and that meditation spot that came up in the last session we did, it's been a lot better. And I discovered a wind chime hanging from the tree on the bank!

3. I've been really torn about taking that job offer overseas. I've felt at a crossroads, you know? If I don't take the job, the higher-ups might figure I'm not dedicated to the firm. On the other hand, I have to consider my relationship with my girlfriend. Can it sustain a long separation? So now, I've decided: I have to trust my gut.

4. I've been a crash dummy, always running headlong into every new adventure. Like the only way I could find out if something was going to work for me was to do it and ask questions later. Now, I realize there is another way. I can rehearse a possibility; I don't need to crash test it!

Section Six

"But don't be satisfied with stories,
How things have gone with others.
Unfold your own myth."

--Rumi

Congratulations are in order! You have now covered the five stages Symbolic Modeling's Frameworks for Change process, learned twelve basic Clean Language questions, added significantly helpful specialized questions, learned to model with REPROCess as a guide, and practiced applying them all.

Section Six is about putting what you have learned together. There are two transcripts here for you to study and activities that invite you to work with them in various ways. I fully anticipate you will find still more ways to work with the transcripts, depending on the skills you, personally, most need to practice.

Scope of Practice

If you have gotten this far with your training, having had experiences as both facilitator and client, you are aware that Clean Language questions and Symbolic Modeling can take you to some very deep, very personal places very quickly, whether that is your intention or not. Thus, it is extremely important that you be aware of your contract with your client and of your training/background. If you do not have a mental health degree or license, you need to be careful that you are not providing *therapy*. For example, if you are a coach and your client asks for help getting clear on a management issue, you may feel it is appropriate to do some metaphor work on "leading at your best." But take care not to stray too deeply into personal background issues that may come up (e.g. major dysfunctional family history). Your client hasn't signed on to address those issues, and you may not be prepared to handle the memories, feelings, or issues that emerge. Your client might willingly go there during the session, compelled by their curiosity or desire to address the issues. But when the session is over, they may be disturbed by how much personal information they have shared in what they expected would be a different sort of relationship.

Differences Between Counseling and Coaching

If, as a coach, you find your client is dealing with severe and persistent sleep problems, depression that makes it difficult to work, high levels of anxiety unwarranted by the circumstances, drug or alcohol abuse, significant low self-esteem issues, or traumatic past memories, it is appropriate for you to recommend counseling or therapy. While this is not an exhaustive list, it gives you an idea of what should be "red flags" for you.

If, as a therapist, you find your client is dealing with challenges developing business strategies, formulating and realizing team goals, setting task priorities, defining their leadership style, or marketing services or products effectively, it is appropriate for you to recommend coaching.

The Symbolic Modeling process is the same for counselor and coach; the difference is in *where you direct your client's attention*. In general, coaches stay focused on desired outcomes and on resources. While these foci are effective for therapists as well, they may also find themselves assisting their clients in healing from past damage and changing dysfunctional coping strategies that are damaging themselves and/or others.

When You Are In Too Deep

There is no one right way or answer as to how to handle this situation, so I am sharing with you my suggestions, based on my experience. If you are not trained in counseling or you do not intend to provide therapy, but you find yourself in what *feels* like "therapeutic content," I suggest the following. (Note: I say *feels* like because, when your client is in metaphor, you can't always tell. Listen to your instincts.)

Step 1: Don't get carried away by your own desire to help.

Licensed clinicians spend literally thousands of hours developing their skills under the direct supervision of experienced mentors. That doesn't, of course, guarantee that they are all wonderful clinicians, but they are experienced in assessing and managing clients and situations that you aren't and may be aware of resources of which you are not. Bringing up a lot of your client's old emotional baggage that you are not prepared to help them handle may leave them insufficiently supported— and risks reinforcing the trauma. Consider, too, that working with you may give them just enough support to get by, and so keep them from seeking help from a professional better able to address their therapeutic needs.

Step 2: Don't cut the session short abruptly.

Hold the space and stick to the process, at least long enough to finish the session gently. Think of a deep-sea diver: you don't want to cause the bends by coming up out of the symbolic domain too quickly. Nor do you want to suggest your client has done something wrong.

Step 3: Head back to a resource state.

Backtrack your way out of the part of the landscape that seems to be laden with intense emotions or memories. Go back to a resource, a feeling of strength or safety, for example, that your client has already mentioned. Then, spend plenty of time there, developing it and letting the client "swim" in that feeling. Then, you may either:

> **Steer the session in a more appropriate direction** (e.g. more about the business plan)
> or
> **Gently end the session with the client in the resource state**

You may want to suggest the client seek other professional help to manage the therapeutic issue, if that seems appropriate. Reiterate what your contract is and what you are prepared to offer. It is an excellent idea to have several therapists you can recommend. It is a good idea to suggest more than one, so the client makes the choice.

New Clients

The suggestions above may also be helpful to the counselor or therapist who is working with a client for the first time. You may sense the client is not yet ready to trust you with highly personal information, and you may choose to keep your first session away from what feel like more emotionally-charged areas until you have established a relationship.

Trauma Survivors

A therapist can also use a backtrack-to-a-resource strategy if a trauma survivor shows signs of being flooded. I do not want to encourage therapists to bail at the first signs of anxiety or tears, but you want to be sure you are masterful enough with Symbolic Modeling that you can handle the many parts of a client's landscape. A client may have one or more *inner children* of varying ages, one or both metaphoric parents, a number of resources, and many other moving parts in a complex landscape of a client dealing with blocked trauma in the system. David Grove first developed Clean Language to work with trauma clients, and CL and SyM are powerful, effective techniques for working with it, but such a client is not one with whom to practice this technique when you are a beginner!

If you, as a novice Symbolic Modeling facilitator, suddenly find yourself in what seems to be a highly emotionally-charged area and you are uncomfortable with your skills, you can use the same backtracking and redirecting technique as a coach to re-direct your client's attention to another part of the landscape (such as a resource) or to another therapeutic approach with which you are more skilled. If you do segue to another technique, be careful to stay *clean* with any information about metaphors that came up, protecting the integrity of the process you were using and respecting your client's metaphoric self-determination. Once you are more experienced, I am confident you will find SyM to be a very effective tool to use with such clients.

Session Transcripts

To clarify the difference between the way a coach and a counselor or therapist might appropriately work, what follows are transcripts of two sessions with the same client. One session directs attention where a business coach would likely go, the other where a counselor or therapist would likely focus.

In order to keep the transcripts reasonably short, I have not included all the repetitions of the client's words as I said them in the sessions nor every question I asked. My intent is to give you a feel for a regular session and how the questions and the five stages weave in and about, and have you follow the logic of the questions. My questions are numbered to make it easier to reference specific ones for study purposes. You may choose to do the suggested Activity 6.1 before you read the session as a whole or after, whichever way you feel works best for you.

6.1 *Activity*

Select one of these next transcripts. Using something to block the facilitator's next question from view, look over each client statement and decide what your next question would be. You could go in any number of directions with any statement. I had to make many choices in the moment, leaving out things I would have liked to explore. Sometimes, my choice was not about something you can read here, but depended on the way the client said something (a word emphasized, a pause taken), or it was because of an intuitive hunch... or, surely, sub-conscious reasons I don't know about. All this is to say, notice what you notice, decide what you decide, and don't think because you choose a different question than I did that you are necessarily wrong. There is room to the right for you to make notes for this and later activities. If you are learning with a trainer or practice partner, the right margin is a good place to note where you have questions or comments.

A Coaching Session

John is a first-time client who has called with a business problem. He's curious to find out if working with metaphors can help. He is a doctor trying to grow his laser eye treatment practice. John has two employees who are not working as a team; they are refusing to even communicate with one another. Not only are the general office atmosphere and morale suffering, but also a lot of money has been wasted on ineffective marketing. With a SyM session, John discovers a new perspective on his dilemma that linear, logical analysis might never have uncovered.

1. And when two employees refusing to communicate, what would you like to have happen?

   John: *I want to be able to take effective action for the problem to get resolved. I need to make a shift in my leadership.*

2. And a shift in your leadership and take effective action. And when effective action, what kind of effective is that effective?

   John: *I want my staff to work as an effective team.*

3. And an effective team and effective action, and a shift in your leadership. And when leadership, what kind of leadership is that leadership, when you take effective action?

   John: *It's a mindset, but there's an internal block. There's a block in my mindset.*

4. And an internal block. And when an internal block in your mindset, where is that block?

   John: *In my middle.*

5. And in your middle. And whereabouts in your middle?

   John: *Above my belly somewhere.*

6. And in the middle, above your belly. And when in the middle, above your belly, where above your belly is that block?

   John: *Hmm.... It's on the outside.*

7. And when a block in the middle, above your belly, on the outside, that's a block like what?

   John: *They're knots. I'm tied in knots. I have mixed feelings.*

8. And mixed feelings and tied in knots. And when knots, in your middle, how many knots could there be?

   John: *About 20 knots, big ones, about the size of two golf balls. They're not easy to untie, but they could unravel easily.*

Such in-the-body metaphors can pop up unexpectedly; what might this have to do with John's business? With a few more questions, John identifies these knots as being about his 3-year-old self. Oh! This sounds like counseling territory. John doesn't want to go there, he says, not yet. Though I am a counselor and John has called me knowing that, he has made his comfort level and desired outcome clear. I immediately decide to treat it like a coaching session. We will stay focused on a present problem and address a practical solution. I won't ignore the knots, but I won't explore them in the depth I would in a counseling session. I have done some development of them already. I have a number, a location, a size, and some information about unraveling. Enough for now. I am not going for a more embodied experience of them than that. I will treat them as a problem (think P/R/O), already sufficiently developed. Clearly, these aren't rules; I am just letting you know about my decision in the moment.

9. And knots. Twenty big ones. And they could unravel easily.

   John: *Huh! Did I say they could unravel easily? Hmm.*

10. And when there are twenty knots in your middle, what would you like to have happen?

    John: *The knots were a stability. They kept things together, in order, intact.*

11. And they were a stability. And when a stability, then what happens?

    John: *At least it works. I mean, the marketing happens. But it doesn't really. It seems like it on the surface. The kn*ots keep things together. But it doesn't really work.

12. And when knots keep things together and it doesn't really work, what would you like to have happen?

    John: *I'd really like things to really work.*

13. And when really work, what kind of really is that really?

    John: *Effortlessly, spontaneously, naturally, without me having to push, to be in there, pulling, pushing. The knots clearly prevent it from working.*

14. And when knots clearly prevent it from working and when knots are a stability, what would you like to have happen?

    John: *Obviously the knots tie it down, hold things in, constrain. Things can't go anywhere. They limit movement and possibilities*

John hasn't answered my question. Instead, he has discovered more information about current conditions. Well and good! I will ask for a desired outcome again, and perhaps now he will have the information he needs in order to know what he wants.

15. And when twenty knots around your middle, on the outside, limit movement and possibilities, what would you like to have happen?

    John: *Well, the obvious thing is to have no knots, but that's not what I really want. What I really want is an effective marketing department that's aligned with and going in the same direction as the business. I don't want the people in that department to be doing their own thing.*

16. And effective and aligned, and going in the same direction. And when aligned, is there anything else about aligned?

    John: *I want to trust that all my employees are working for the good of the business.*

John has popped out of his symbolic domain, leaving the knots and going back to talking about the business. That's fine; all part of his system. But working with his metaphors seems promising. I had inched back toward them by asking about the word *aligned*, possibly an embedded metaphor. But John didn't respond to that invitation. I will be more overt this time in directing his attention toward his metaphors again. I could go back to *aligned*, but something in John's tone draws me to the word *trust*.

17. And when trust that all are working for the good, that's trust like what?

    John: *I'm reminded of a movie about a rugby team, "Forever Strong." It was about a coach who really inspired his team. All the members worked together, committed to each other, and kept working for the same goal.*

18. And "Forever Strong." And what kind of strong was that strong?

    John: *It was an internal strength. And what was critical is they had this coach who stood for certain things. Sometimes people didn't understand, but they stood for the same values or they didn't survive on the team. No two ways about it. The coach had one agenda. Two agendas don't work.*

19. And is there a relationship between a coach with one agenda and values and inspired...and an effective marketing team?

    John: *There is a difference, and maybe there isn't. The trouble is I can't say I'm an expert in marketing. It's not my expertise. A sports coach is an expert in the sport he coaches. He's played it himself; he knows the game. I'm setting an example in leading, but I can't be a marketing director. How could I be an effective coach when I don't have the expertise? My mind says it's something else.*

20. And when an effective coach doesn't have the expertise, that's an effective coach like what?

    John: See, that's the distinction between rugby and Aikido. In Aikido there's a standard way of doing things. All someone has to do is learn the skill, and you can coach someone else. You don't have to be a world expert. But what I do is different. It's a more creative thing. No one knows the answer until it unfolds. No one is the expert.... I think my knots are the belief that I have to be the expert.

John refers back to a metaphor he mentioned earlier, his knots, which just shows you how a client's metaphors are all active in his system, whether you are hearing about them or not. I give John a moment or two to sit with his interpretation, but I don't pursue the knot reference. I stick to my decision not to delve further into a metaphor that John has expressly said he was not ready to explore. Instead, I repeat a variation of my last question.

21. And what you do is a creative thing, and no one is the expert. And what kind of a coach is a coach who's not an expert and does a creative thing?

John is quiet for some time. I spend the minute musing on what I could ask next, since this question seems to be stumping John. But, no. He finds his resourceful metaphor.

22. John: *I'm like the director of a movie. We don't know all the answers. We have scripts, and we have an idea of the way it should go. The director ultimately determines the direction. Decisions have to be made. You can't have everyone be the director.*

23. And the director of a movie and don't know all the answers. And when decisions have to be made, then what happens?

    John: *Sometimes you make good ones, sometimes bad ones. That's life when you make creative decisions.*

Our time is about up. Has this new awareness caused a change that reverberates through the system? I begin maturing, this time "touching lightly" on the knots.

24. And when that's life, and you can't have everyone be the director, and no one is the expert, what happens to knots around your middle that limit possibilities?

    John: If I shift, I'll know it. I'll be able to take effective action.

I notice John has said "if I shift," so it hasn't happened yet. I decide to let his system integrate the new knowledge it has and leave off working with it outright. John begins talking about specific employees on his team, assessing their strengths and weaknesses. He doesn't mention the knots, and I follow his lead, focusing on how to apply in practice what he has gained from his film director metaphor.

John: *I want to build a marketing team, aligned with the business, that's able to learn and grow.*

24. And when build a marketing team, what needs to happen for that marketing team to be aligned with the business?

John lists four indications that will tell him the team is aligned, and we explore in practical ways, using CLQs, what it will take to build a team like that. To implement these, more potential business issues arise for John to consider, but he contends nonetheless that, "This is a great place to be." He leaves with what will hopefully be an empowering metaphor, himself as a film director, and a new perspective on his role and his team.

And the knots? I chose not to direct him back to consider them. The conversation had taken a more business-oriented focus, and John was no longer in his symbolic domain. Earlier, he sensed the knots were still serving a purpose. I will honor his mind/body's wisdom that the knots need to be there for now, however constraining, and leave them to another session or to the power of the metaphor work we did today to affect this part of John's system. Maybe they will "unravel easily."

My take-away from this section is...

Questions I have...

A Counseling Session

John came back a week later. You may wonder, will the film director be a part of this session? Will the knots still be there? Sometimes, metaphors reappear, sometimes they evolve, sometimes themes or patterns emerge. Here's what happened.

1. And is there anything else about your session last week?

   John: *I've shifted. I thought I had to know everything. At work, I've noticed a difference in myself, and I think others have noticed, too.*

Then, John dismisses that topic. He has called about a different, more personal issue, he says, something he would like to work on for himself. Because I trust the Clean process and because I trust the client to be the expert on himself, I do not substitute my agenda for his or let my curiosity about the effects of last week's session drive this session.

We look at John's Before Our Session sheet. He has drawn two simple stick figure portraits of himself, both facing to the right and walking forward with outstretched arms. The only obvious difference between them is the one labeled "now" has a pot belly. John has written:

> John: *I would like to lose weight and have a smaller, flatter stomach. I would like the loss of weight to result in a much healthier, more active me.*

Assuring John that he is welcome to change and/or add to what he has written in any way that seems appropriate now, I have him read his words aloud. This way, he actively puts these exact words into the session and enables me to hear his voice tone and emphasis. As John reads, I do something out of the ordinary. I am struck by his repetition of the phrase "I would like..." at the start of both sentences. Something about the way he says these words and their repetition compels me to start with his desiring rather than his outcomes. I will come back to the outcomes later.

2. And when you'd like to lose weight...and flatter stomach...and you'd like a healthier, more active you, what kind of like is that like?

   John: *Ah, interesting question. It's a want. It's a desire, and I don't want it to destroy me. I'm so driven for the goal that I can't be me.*

3. And what would you like to have happen when it's a desire, and you're so driven for the goal that you can't be you?

John: *I'd like the want to be so aligned—so much a part of me—that it naturally changes. The things I say I want, to be healthier and slimmer, I want them to be congruent with my behavior.*

There's that word *aligned* again. It came up frequently in John's last session. This seems to be a recurrent concept in his system, and I want to help John explore what aligned means for him.

4. And congruent and aligned. And is there anything else about that aligned?

   John: *If I'm aligned, I won't have to protect myself. There's a fear, near the heart, of not having enough, fear of greed... fear "I can't leave it or I won't get my share."*

I had planned to get a metaphor for aligned, but like an unanticipated chess move, John has introduced something new. Because he describes a new awareness in his body, I abandon my plan for now and ask instead about the problem, which reveals a resource put in place long ago:

5. And when a fear near your heart, whereabouts near your heart?

   John: *It's like I'm holding on to something. Something is a protection.*

6. And a protection. And when a protection near your heart, that's a protection like what?

   John: *Like a steel plate that things bounce off of.*

7. And a steel plate things bounce off of. And whereabouts is that steel plate?

   John: *On the outside, in front of my abdomen.*

8. And when a steel plate, in front of your abdomen, whereabouts in front is that plate?

   John: *It's two inches in front of me. And I'm hiding.*

9. And two inches in front, and you're hiding. And is there a relationship between fear and not getting enough, near the heart, and steel plate two inches in front of you?

John: *Yes, it anchors. It attaches to the steel plate. It holds it.*

10. And attaches and holds it… like what?

    John: *Like it's welded, solid and stiff. It reminds me of the snow plows we'd attach to the front of trucks in winter where I grew up. We had lots of snow.*

11. And when fear in your heart, and it's welded to the steel plate, what would you like to have happen?

    John: *I'd like to remove the snow plow, like it's summer now, and they remove the plow.*

12. And what needs to happen for you to remove the snow plow?

    John: *The season changes, so it's no longer needed. Here, fear of greed is no longer needed.*

13. And when fear of greed is no longer needed and the season changes, can snow plow be removed?

    John: (pause) *Ask me again. Sorry, I was gone.*

It would be so easy to dismiss this statement as an interruption, a throw-away line in John's narrative. But, I wonder, where was it John went?

14. And when you were gone, where were you gone to?

    John: *A peaceful place. Time stops there; I'm sleepy but not sleepy. I'm calm.*

I am not sure what this place has to do with John's desired outcomes or his steel plates. But if it has come up now, I trust this place is a related part of John's system, and it sounds like it could be a resource. I will help him explore it.

15. And is there anything else about that peaceful place?

    John: *I was somewhere the plow was no longer needed. Spring in my hometown. It's warm and comfortable. There's sun. It's calm.*

16. And spring in your hometown. Warm, comfortable, calm. And when it's spring, and the plow is no longer needed, then what happens?

    John: *I'm relaxed and can be present. I can enjoy the changes in my body, enjoy sights and sounds.*

17. And where is that peaceful place you were gone to?

    John: *It's on the inside, around my head and upper chest.*

I notice that this peaceful place is in John's head and his upper chest—perhaps near the fear around his heart place? I'm wondering how these might relate.

18. And a peaceful place and it's warm...and sun…and you're relaxed and can enjoy changes. And when you're in that peaceful place, what happens to near the heart?

    John: *There was a holding on and a weld. Yes, stiff and unbending.*

19. And when you go to a peaceful place in head and upper chest, what happens to that weld?

    John: *It isn't holding on anymore.*

20. And it isn't holding on anymore. And when weld isn't holding on anymore, then what happens?

    John: *It can be part of the peaceful place, and the peaceful place expands.*

21. And as the peaceful place expands, what happens to heart?

    John: *It's more included. It's still somewhat on the edge, but it's definitely in.*

I am not sure if this is a problem. Is John okay with his heart being on the edge?

22. And when it's definitely in, and it's still somewhat on the edge, what would you like to have happen?

    John: *The heart is more the center now, the focus. The peaceful place is much larger now and includes the stomach. Though there's some resistance there.*

I am reminded of the knots, but decide for now that rather than asking about the resistance and focusing on the problem, I will develop this calm, relaxed feeling in this peaceful place—still a fairly new resource—and see what bringing more awareness to it might do to the resistance.

23. And what kind of focus is that focus when heart is more the center, the focus, of the peaceful place?

    John: *It's a soft focus.*

24. And a soft focus. And when soft, what kind of soft is that soft?

    John: *It's understanding, compassionate, accepting, loving.*

25. And when understanding, is there anything else about that understanding?

    John: *It's expansive, not intellectual.*

26. And when a focus is soft, understanding, compassionate, accepting, loving, expansive, where could a focus like that come from?

    John: *It was always there. It was just protected and hidden.*

27. And when a soft focus is always there in the center of a peaceful place, and it's compassionate and loving, what difference does knowing that make?

    John: *Now it's effortless, more aligned, peaceful, encompassing, expansive, more inclusive.*

Once John confirms all these changes, and I give him some more time to register these feelings, I am ready to check in on the stomach, recalling how he started with resistance and his desired outcome to have a flatter stomach.

28. And when a peaceful place...and head...and upper chest…and heart the focus…and includes the stomach…and now it's effortless…more aligned...more inclusive, what happens to stomach?

    John: *It's included. It's softer. It's part of that place, and it's more powerful.*

29. And part of that place. And more powerful. And what kind of powerful is that powerful?

    John: *It's trusting. It's relentlessly powerful.*

30. And when it's relentlessly powerful, that's relentlessly powerful like what?

    John: *Like flowing water.*

31. And flowing water. And is there anything else about that flowing water?

    John: *Yes...it's clear, clean, fresh. And it's cold.*

32. And cold, fresh, clean, clear, flowing water. And when flowing, what kind of flowing is that flowing?

    John: *It's a stream flowing over the rocks, around the rocks.*

33. And a stream, flowing over, around the rocks. And is there anything else about that flowing stream?

    John: *The sun sparkles on it, and nothing stops it.*

34. And when a flowing stream, over and around rocks and nothing stops it, whereabouts could flowing like that come from?

    John: *From the heart. It's an endless supply.*

35. And from the heart. An endless supply. And when nothing stops it and it's an endless supply, what difference does knowing that make?

    John: *It can't be dammed up. Well, it could be, but it's not. And it's fresh tasting.*

36. And is there a relationship between a relentlessly powerful flow of water, clean and fresh, from the heart and includes the stomach, and endless supply...and a healthier you?

    John: *Oh, wow! Yes!! That is healthy!*

37. And a stomach that's softer and more powerful and trusting. And what kind of trusting is that trusting?

    John: *It's letting the water flow. The water is pure, clean. There are fish in it. It's crystal clear, peaceful yet vibrant. There's energy there.*

38. And energy there. And what kind of energy is that energy?

    John: *It's rippling, dancing, water over the rocks, heading downhill, along the stream.*

It sounds like lots of movement, lots of action. It makes me think of one of John's initial desired outcomes, to be more active, so I check to see if there is a relationship.

39. And when a rippling, dancing energy, is there a relationship between energy like that and a more active you?

    John: *Yes!*

40. And what kind of active you is that active you?

    John: *It's me without the steel plate, more flowing, less holding.*

Had you forgotten all about the steel plate? John hadn't. It was all part of his system. I review the highlights of all the changes he has noted, and go back again to his first statement.

41. And when all that, what happens to lose weight and a healthier, more active you?

    John: *It is. The stream just is. It doesn't need to look like anything.*

It sounds like a new John, a John with a very different sense of self. I am wondering what this John wants.

42. And when a stream just is, and it doesn't need to look like anything, what would you like to have happen?

    John: *I want the stream to nourish all aspects of my life, business, personal, creative, physical, relationships.*

43. And what needs to happen for the stream to nourish all that?

    John: *The water just needs to flow.*

44. And is there anything else that needs to happen?

    John: *It just has to come from the source.*

45. And come from the source. And whereabouts is that source?

    John: *The source is a magical place, a special place....I'm seeing a place.*

46. And a magical place, a special place. And whereabouts is that place?

    John: *I'm seeing a place near my heart. There, out of the rocks, comes water. It's special.*

47. And what kind of special is that special?

    John: *It's cold, clear, wonderful tasting.*

48. And water, cold, clear, wonderful tasting. And can water like that flow endlessly from that magic place near your heart?

    John: *Yes*!

49. And take all the time you need to become more and more familiar with that endlessly flowing water from the source, from that magical place, from a stream that nourishes. From the heart. And a healthier, more active you.

This is where the session ended. John released the protection that no longer served. The old resource, the snow plow, is gone. Perhaps these were the knots from the last session in another guise; I don't know, and I decide not to ask. I don't want to impose on my client's moving experience by asking him questions to satisfy my curiosity. As a facilitator, you will never be privileged enough to know all about your client's metaphor landscape, and you have to be comfortable with that.

With more time we could have done more maturing. But our time is up. John has discovered new resources: a peaceful place where he can relax and flowing water that nourishes all aspects of his life. I invite John to draw a metaphor map when he has an opportunity, so he can revisit what he has discovered and get to know it all better.

My take-away from this section is...

Questions I have...

6.2 *Activity*

Go through the session transcripts, and identify resources with an (**R**) in the right margin. What do you notice?

6.3 *Activity*

Go back through one or both session transcripts and identify examples of the following using these labels:

1. The client's problem (**P**), remedy (**R**), and desired outcome (**DO**) statements
2. Conditions needed for change (**C for C**)
3. When a change occurs (**C**)
4. When maturing (**M**) occurs

Notice, sometimes these will be as a result of the facilitator's questions. Sometimes, the client does them for himself.

6.4 *Activity*

With your client or practice partner's permission, tape a session or portion of a session, and type up a transcript of about 10 minutes of it. Or use a transcription service; there are numerous ones on the Internet, some free, though you will want to review the transcript for accuracy.

- Examine your question choices, and now, with all the time you want to review your client's words, consider what else you might liked to have asked and why.
- You can do the same 6.2 and 6.3 activities with your transcript.
- The transcript also makes it much easier to deconstruct a session for yourself or to discuss with a practice partner or a consulting trainer like myself than if you use a recording. I recommend numbering statements or questions, as it makes it much easier to keep track of where you are or what you want to refer to.

FAQ Frequently Asked Questions

What if my client brings up real life memories?

What if your client shifts from the symbolic domain to telling you about a real life memory? If your client has been deep in symbolic work, it is unlikely this memory has popped up randomly. There may be some helpful information there, though you could likely categorize much of it as an Explanation.

Some facilitators will cut off descriptions of past events quickly and immediately lead a client back to the symbolic domain, electing to "do the work" there. Others will let the memory emerge, looking for new information, insight or direction, which they will then guide into metaphor and begin modeling again, seeking connections to the existing landscape.

You will no doubt experiment and find the way that works for you and your client. Keep in mind you and your client have a limited amount of time and energy, so use it in what you sense is the most productive way for your client. Some helpful things you might be listening for are:

- A pattern of which they hadn't been aware
- A forgotten resource that they have been unable to access or use in the past
- A related problem that you could ask a desired outcome for

For these reasons, I personally tend to let the memory emerge for my clients for a brief time. I am very quick to redirect them with a review and CLQs if they start telling me details of someone else's part of their story.

What if my client says, "I don't know"?

Many times when a client says, "I don't know," what they really mean is "I don't know yet." First, try waiting patiently, perhaps just reviewing a bit of the information. Or just look patient and expectant. Often, what the client really needs is simply time to figure it out.

Sometimes, "I don't know" means "I don't have enough information." You can then help your client develop more details about their space and symbols with CLQs. Helpful new information may emerge. Or it may not; your client may not be able to access more information at this time.

You may have asked an awkwardly worded question, jumped in metaphoric time or space, or in some other way asked for too great a leap on the part of your client. No need for explanations or apologies; these are distractions. Just review and ask another simple CLQ about what is most present for the client in the moment, and get back on track.

It may suit the logic of the landscape to explore the client's not knowing as a problem.

Example:

Client:	Since I was young, my parents pushed me to be successful, and I want to be successful!
Facilitator:	And your parents pushed you to be successful. And you want to be successful! And is that the same successful or different successful?
Client:	I don't really know. Hmm....
Facilitator:	And when you don't really know, what would you like to have happen?
Client:	I'd like to know for sure what successful for me is.
Facilitator:	And you'd like to know for sure what successful for you is. And when you know for sure, whereabouts is that know?
Client:	It's in my gut, deep in my gut.

I find it is often significant for clients to locate their knowing, to discover whether it comes from themselves or from someone or something else. I have had many clients realize they are waiting for their knowing to come from someone else (e.g. answers to "What should I do about with my career? My relationship? My disappointment?") If they hear themselves say aloud that they are waiting for someone else to tell them, their adult conscious selves may be quick to say, "But I know the answer has to come from me." Often, they return to their metaphor landscape with a new awareness and determination.

With the client above, you could develop a metaphor for "know for sure in [their] gut" and, with that resource in awareness, then find out more about what successful is for them. And even if the knowing your client wants/needs isn't available to them, valuable information may emerge about how they handle not knowing. You will learn something about their patterns, and so may they. Stay with the process; keep asking CLQs.

Be patient. Something always happens!

Are there times I should explore the negative?

In Symbolic Modeling, we generally focus on the desired outcome. But sometimes you need to find out a bit about a symbol that appears to be a problem. (Notice I avoid the word negative. Remember latent resources? You can't always tell what will be positive and what will be negative!) As a rule of thumb, the problem needs to be addressed when your client keeps coming back to it despite your directing their attention repeatedly to an outcome or when it is clearly impeding progress towards the desired outcome, especially if they are already in the symbolic domain, like John was.

In such cases, you want to find out enough about the attributes and the location of the symbol so that the logic of how to deal with it emerges. For example, suppose there's something squeezing the client's chest, painfully. If it is a rope, the client may realize they can cut it. If they are squeezing hands, whose are they and what do they want to have happen? If it is a python…and so on. In other words, you may need to collect some information to help the client determine their relevant desired outcome, the necessary conditions for change, and/or what sort of resource to look for. I think of it as developing a symbol *lightly*.

What you don't need to do is hold attention on the *painfully* in the above example. Why would that be useful for the client to know more about? You would just be encouraging an embodied experience of a disempowered state.

Are there times I shouldn't stay with Clean Language?

Some examples of when to stop using your CLQs might include times when:

- Your client is confused by the SyM process, and some explanation is in order
- Your client makes eye contact and speaks to you directly in a cognitive way
- Your client's initial desired outcome is clearly harmful to himself or others (When you're dealing with metaphoric desired outcomes, that's different.)

Use your common sense! As you become more familiar with what Clean Language can do, you will be more comfortable with when it may not be appropriate to stick with. But you needn't bail out just because you and/or your client is at a loss. I think of such moments as being right where we need to be: on the edge of what we already know, ready to discover what we don't know. Trust the process!

What if my client gets upset or panicky?

Don't pull the plug at the first sign of tears or distress. These are often learning moments, and what your client most needs is your patience and expectation that tears and discomfort are not to be automatically fled from. Your calm presence will be reassuring.

That said, a mind/body flooded or highly defensive is not open to new learning. Neither do you want to leave your client in panic or misery. Should you sense that your client needs some centering in order to be able to keep reprocessing, you can backtrack to a resource state or symbol.

Facilitator: And when you're frightened, what happens just before you're frightened?
And when you're frightened, is there anything else about Tin Man with his axe?

If your client is enacting or physicalizing the metaphor landscape, you could direct them to move themselves or their attention to a space or symbol away from the frightening space where they can reconsider it from a safer distance/perspective. You could offer a generic invitation, directing, "And find another space… where you would like to be…. And what do you know from there?"

If your client becomes upset to an extent that they are likely to disengage from the process or get panicky, if they seem to be so distracted as to not be able to hear you, you can be more conversational and reassuring, deliberately pulling away from the symbolic domain, with grounding phrases like:

- "Remember, I'm going to ask you, 'And what would you like to have happen?'" (emphasizing the client's control in the moment; giving them a chance to get ready for the question itself)
- "Remember, I'm right here with you/We're here in this room together."

You can also refer to your client by name, which tends to bring them out from their inner focus a bit. When the client resumes exploring, go slowly. Be careful you are not rushing your client to change.

Most people are predominantly visual. Does Symbolic Modeling work best for them, and not so much for others?

While 60-70% of people are identified as predominantly visual, as far as I know, with the exception of those who have been blind since birth who dream with only a dialogue going on in their minds, like some sort of radio show, everyone else dreams in images that play along with the words. So, while the visual mode may not be dominant for everyone, it is certainly familiar to them, and it seems to be a common way our subconscious minds work and express themselves. Which is why it makes so much sense to be working with symbols and images, the language of the subconscious, and not with words alone.

I recall a client who told me he didn't see images; he thought in terms of vibrations. So we worked with vibrations for the first two sessions. During his third session, his landscape "went visual." I had no intent for that to happen; there was no reason to suppose that that was any better or worse a way of working than with vibrations. And I don't know what significance the shift had. It is just what happened.

The key is to honor your client's way of working. Invoke David Grove's creative spirit, invite your client to play, and experiment! Recall what you learned about enacting and physicalizing metaphor landscapes. Non-visually dominant clients may like a more kinesthetic approach such as moving in space or using their hands to draw.

6.5 *Activity*

Time for practice with a partner or client. Plan on 30-40 minutes per client so you have time to develop information and work with it. Or you may want to continue developing a landscape that you already have information about so that you are more likely to move quickly to Stages 4 and 5: Establishing Conditions for Change and Maturing Change.

Afterward, answer the following questions:

Something I did well was:

Something I want to work on next time is:

Symbolic Modeling at a Distance

While I prefer to work with a client in person, sometimes that's not possible. A Clean Language session can be successfully conducted from a distance, yet there are certain differences from doing one in person. While *every* Clean Language client partners with the facilitator in the process, this is especially true when you are not in the same room with one another.[4]

If you can have a video connection, it is certainly preferable to a phone, as being able to see your client helps you pick up nonverbal clues and time your questions appropriately. If it is not possible to see your client, consider how you will prepare them. No doubt you will find your own way, but, if it is helpful to you, here are the things I cover at the start of our first session.

I email a Client Information form and a *Before Our Session* sheet ahead of time. The latter I encourage them to fill close to the time of the session, so it contains what's up for them in the moment; even so, I will invite them to add or change what they have when the time comes to describe it. Then I let them know...

You will need:

- a quiet space where you can be undisturbed for _____ minutes
- paper and markers, in case you will want to make a sketch of your metaphors
- some Post-it notes of various colors

I will be asking simple questions using your exact words so you can hear them again, notice what you notice, and respond with what comes up for you.

While my questions have a purpose, I can't know what you're experiencing. Once we get into the symbolic domain—the landscape of your metaphors—you may have a sense about what things draw your attention, what you want to explore. Let me know where your intuition is leading you, and I will follow.

Any questions before we begin?

If I cannot see the client, I encourage them in advance to let me know if I am timing my questions too fast or too slowly. Usually, it doesn't take long to establish a rhythm.

If the client can see me, I explain I will be taking notes to be sure I have their exact words to refer to, so as to reassure them that I am not labeling or noting judgments of any kind. And I let them know before we start that I will be keeping minimal eye contact, because this isn't like a normal conversation. Clients like my phrase, "This is about self-exploration, not self-explanation."

Mixing CL and SyM with Other Approaches

You can use CLQs and/or SyM strategies in other contexts altogether. You can mix Clean and non-clean questions and statements. You can think P/R/O. You can use maturing strategies with any conclusion reached. In other words, you can apply these *techniques* to other ways of working.

What I am not encouraging you to do is to integrate other techniques into a Symbolic Modeling session. Grove's CL and Tompkins and Lawley's SyM strategies for using CL have elegant structures and very carefully delineated parameters. It is difficult to integrate another way of working into a SyM session and be true to this deeply respectful, Clean way of working.

You could, however, make a CL or SyM session part of a longer meeting with your client where you do other work as well.

- You can let the SyM session and the other work stand as two discreet parts of what you are doing.
- You can take the information that emerges in the SyM session and work with it in a different way.

But this second approach, integrating the content, is tricky! Remember to stay *clean* with the information that emerges in a Symbolic Modeling session. I am confident at this point that you will not offer suggestions as to what to do with a metaphor's problem.

Also, be careful not to interpret the metaphors, even if your client starts to interpret for themselves or asks for your insights.

When my clients do start interpreting, I don't want to suggest they are doing something wrong, but I gently suggest it is not likely to be helpful. Their metaphors could well stand for any number of things, and interpreting them puts them into "little boxes" that may not be accurate and may restrict how the client consciously thinks about them. I generally find clients seem relieved to be unburdened from what they thought they should be doing. Respect the metaphors' sanctity (and they do feel sacred, for they feel so deeply, so profoundly true) and let them simply be themselves. If you do refer to them, be sure to use your client's exact words.

To give you an example of using content from a SyM session with another technique cleanly, sometimes I invite a client to choose a statement from our session to use in a brief tapping (EFT) session.[5]

Remember, if your client has been working in metaphor in a deeply mindful state, it can feel abrupt and disorienting to do analytical assessments or planning, so take that into consideration when planning to follow a session with another activity or technique.

Choosing the bottom-up approach

One of the most valuable aspects of working with Clean Language and Symbolic Modeling is their bottom-up approach. That is, they start at the grass roots by helping a client answer fundamental questions: "Who am I, and what do I want?" Many other ways of working with clients are top-down approaches. These say, "Here's a wonderful inventory or theory that will reveal much about you, that can tell you what is right for you or that can diagnose you and/or your problem. This survey/I will determine which box or boxes you fit in." or "Now that I've assessed your problem/situation/self, I can suggest how best to fix things."

CL and SyM start with the premise that if you only look at certain boxes, you will most likely miss information not pertaining to those boxes. And you will be making lots of assumptions. And you will be less accurate and less effective than you might realize. And there is another way!

6.6 *Activity*

Your Elevator Speech: I expect by now you are eagerly sharing what you are learning here with others. How do you describe Clean Language and Symbolic Modeling? Record in the space below and on the next page what you will say if you only have a minute or two (the typical length of an elevator ride). Share with your practice buddy.

Key points about Clean Language:

Key points about Symbolic Modeling:

My **metaphor** for the way they work:

CL and SyM are particularly valuable tools for the work I do because:

Section Six Summary

The difference between **coaching** and **counseling** with Symbolic Modeling is where you, the facilitator, direct attention.

Always keep your client's best interest in mind and practice within **your scope of expertise**.

If you are getting "in too deep," **backtrack to a resource state** and spend some time there before you redirect your client's attention or end the session.

If you choose to work using a **phone or video connection**, you can conduct a Symbolic Modeling session with some special preparation.

CLQs and **SyM strategies** can be applied to many other approaches and techniques.

My take-away from this section is...

Questions I have...

6.7 *Review Activity*

These are the sorts of statements a client might make to any number of types of healing professionals. But remember: while the CLQs you use and the SyM strategies you employ are the same regardless of your profession, *where you direct your client's attention* may differ, depending on your contract with your client. For this practice activity, decide what you would want to focus on in the following statements and plan what you would ask, using the **REPROC**ess model.

1. I've been unhappy in my job a long time, years in fact, but I just don't know what else I want to do. I've got hobbies, that sort of thing, but nothing I could really make a career out of. I just feel stuck, and it causes me a lot of stress.

2. I wish I could really open my heart to the people in my life. Not everyone of course, but the people I really care about: some co-workers, friends, family. I'd like to be present, to be sensitive to their needs and mindful of how we can best connect with one another.

3. I'm getting ready to retire, and I'm looking forward to getting away from the 9–5 routine. I want to embrace this new phase of my life and have a deep sense of renewal. I might even get a part time job, try something completely new. Like they say, the best is yet to come!

4. I'm a stay-at home parent with three kids under age 10. They're actually wonderful kids, and my spouse is really supportive, but I just feel like everyone wants a part of me. And I want to really embrace and participate in this stage of my kids' lives. But it just feels like there's no part of *me* left for *me*!

Commencement

Completing your introduction to the basic Clean Language questions and the Symbolic Modeling strategies we set out to explore marks both an end and a new beginning. How will you take what you know out into the world?

The key to making the most of what you have learned is to **practice** and **experiment** applying it!

Remember: it is not a question of all or nothing. You do not need to do a full-out Symbolic Modeling session to practice. You can do as few or as many of these as you like:

- Check your assumptions.
- Ask a few CLQs.
- Reference your client's exact words.
- Ask about a metaphor in a conversational manner—*cleanly*.
- Use P/R/O assessing.
- Ask for conditions for change.
- Mature the effects of a change.

Wherever you are with your skills, start there and **set a goal** to incorporate more and more of this material as you are ready.

I would also like to encourage you to **revisit these pages again and again**. I think you will rediscover information and insights that will take on greater significance as your skills and experiences multiply.

Final Activity

My immediate goals related to CL and SyM are:

To accomplish these, the first three specific steps I will take are:

1.

2.

3.

May Clean Language and Symbolic Modeling
enrich your work and your life many times over!

What's Next

YOUR OWN SYMBOLIC MODELING SESSION

If you haven't already experienced a personal, full-on Symbolic Modeling session (by which I mean being facilitated by someone other than another trainee), this is a good next step to fully appreciate what the full process feels like and can do. You can arrange for a sample session by contacting me at gina@cleanlanguageresources.com

TRAINING

Visit my website, www.cleanlanguageresources.com for information about online and in-person training opportunities, workshops, and certification. If nothing convenient for you is on the calendar, contact me at to let me know of your interest. I strongly encourage you to get at least some live training if you want to master the art of Symbolic Modeling, whether it is with me or another experienced trainer. You will get personal coaching and feedback, and you will have a chance to be a client, from which you will learn a great deal about facilitation. And you will make some new friends who are as enthusiastic about Clean as you are!

Resources

MORE READING

About Clean Language and Symbolic Modeling

Campbell, Gina, *Mining Your Client's Metaphors: a How-To Workbook on Clean Language and Symbolic Modeling Basics Part One: Facilitating Clarity*. Balboa Press (Bloomington, IN, 2012, revised 2021)

Campbell, Gina. *Panning for your Client's Gold: 12 Lean Clean Language Processes*. Balboa Press (Bloomington, IN, 2015)

Campbell, Gina. *Hope in a Corner of My Heart: A healing journey through the dream-logical world of inner metaphors*. Balboa Press (Bloomington, IN, 2018)

Cooper, Lynn and Mariette Castellino, *The Five-Minute Coach: Improve Performance Rapidly*, Crown House Publishing Ltd. (Carmarthen, Wales, 2012)

Dunbar, Angela. *Clean Coaching: an insider's guide to making change happen.* Routledge (Oxon, 2017)

Harland, Philip, *Trust Me, I'm the Patient: Clean Language, Metaphor, and the New Psychology of Change*, Wayfinder Press (London, 2012)

Lawley, James and Penny Tompkins, *Metaphors in Mind: Transformation through Symbolic Modelling*, The Developing Company (London, 2000)

Pole, Nick. *Words that Touch: How to ask questions your body can answer (12 essential Clean Questions for mind/body therapists)* Singing Dragon (London, 2017)

Way, Marian. *Clean Approaches for Coaches: how to create the conditions for change using Clean Language and Symbolic Modelling*. Clean Publishing (Hampshire, England, 2013)

Wilson, Carol. *The Work and Life of David Grove: Clean Language and Emergent Knowledge.* Matador (Leicestershire, England, 2017)

References and Footnotes

REFERENCES

Harland, Philip, *Trust Me, I'm the Patient: Clean Language, Metaphor, and the New Psychology of Change*, Wayfinder Press (London, 2012)

Lawley, James and Penny Tompkins, *Metaphors in Mind: Transformation through Symbolic Modeling*, The Developing Company (London, 2000)

REFERENCES FOR QUOTATIONS

Section One: Lakoff, George and Mark Johnson, *Metaphors We Live By*, University of Chicago (Chicago, 1980), p. 233

Section Two: Virginia Satir (1916–1988)

Section Three: Dana Gioia, excerpt from "Words" from *Interrogations at Noon*. Copyright © 2001 by Dana Gioia. Reprinted with permission of The Permissions Company, Inc. on behalf of Graywolf Press, Minneapolis, Minnesota.

Answers to Activities

Activity 1.1

Spot the metaphors. Note that you may not have marked ones I have, and vice versa. What suggests an image or a comparison may differ from person to person, including you and your client. *Directing your client's attention to implied metaphors is not about being clever or tricky; it is about being helpful.* Look for the words likely to be relevant to your client in their context. If you have a practice partner, it is fun to discuss what you noticed.

1. I realize now that my expectations were sky high. It's little wonder I was getting nowhere. Time to get my feet back on the ground and learn to live within my budget constraints. I'm sure I can find a house I'll like if I let go of that ideal image I've been fixated on.

2. Getting myself motivated to actually start a new project is always the hardest part for me. Once I'm out of the starting gate, the momentum carries me. And each item accomplished just spurs me on to add still another.

3. It seemed like a good idea at the time, but now I'm waffling. We've got a great committee assembled, but they're all so strong-willed. It may be that we have too many commanders and not enough sailors to just man the oars. How do we get out of this one?

4. I've come to a fork in the road. Deciding which way to go is tearing me apart! Ask me which way I want to go. One day, I'm sure I should major in engineering. But the next day, I'm equally sure I should study economics—though just what I'd do with that degree is not so clear.

5. I'm overwhelmed by the clutter in my office! Every pile demands my attention, and I'm stressed that something important has gotten buried somewhere, and I'm going to miss an important deadline.

Activity 4.5

Did you identify these outcomes?

1. Be active in a relaxed way. Be more playful. (Note: It is the client's wife, not he, who wants him to take it easy more. He may agree with that as a goal, or he may not. Make no assumptions!)

2. Feel more flexible about how I respond.

3. Be more accepting [of] self. Be more compassionate with self.

4. First sentence: still a remedy; the Desired Outcome is not clear. Motivate myself. Find healthy ways to get out of difficult situations.

5. Stay calm. Talk openly. Talk honestly.

Activity 4.7

Did you identify these desired outcomes? If you or your practice buddy play the client, more may quickly emerge, as there were plenty of problems described.

1. Have a meeting of the minds.

2. (None clearly stated.)

3. Know I'm good enough to be really great at something.

4. (None clearly stated.)

5. Implied: time to myself.

Glossary of Terms

attributes: characteristics of an object, person, place, etc.

backtracking: a facilitator repeats previously given information in reverse order to smoothly direct the attention of a client to a previously mentioned word or image in order to ask a question about it.

bottom-up approach/technique: a counseling or coaching strategy that makes no assumptions (or as few as humanly possible), applies no categories, and works from the ground up with open-ended exploration. A view of the client's system emerges from the details and their interactions.

choice point: a moment or place at which a client has the opportunity to choose among options.

clean: refers to when a facilitator uses primarily a client's exact words and gestures and adheres to the inherent logic of their metaphors. Thus, a "clean question" uses only a bare bones structure of words that are not the client's. "Staying clean" means the facilitator offers no advice, interpretations, rephrasing, or reframing.

Clean Language: the special questions and syntax originally developed by counseling psychologist David Grove to encourage clients to explore their metaphors and inner worlds in order to better know themselves.

Clean Language syntax: the word order/wording of a Clean Language question. What is called full syntax consists of three parts: the repetition of the client's words for acknowledgment, the narrowing of those words to the ones their attention will be directed towards, and the question itself.

Conditions for Change: Stage 4 of the Symbolic Modeling process. What emerges is what a client or symbol needs to happen in order for a desired change to occur.

Desired Outcome: what the client wants and does not currently have.

dream logic: this is my (Gina's) own term for the inherent logic of a client's landscape. It may have its own rules of cause-and-effect, physics, time and space, and so forth that are not consistent with everyday reality. It is more like what often happens in dreams: things suddenly appear and disappear, people morph into other people, animals talk, people fly. Anything can happen!

embedded metaphors: words that suggest an image, object, or comparison not immediately noticeable to most people. Words that may have originally been easily spotted as overt metaphors have become so familiar that we easily overlook their references to other experiences (e.g. She *noted* the cap he had on. It's *beyond* comprehension.)

embodied metaphors: these metaphors compare one thing to something experienced by a physical being in a physical world. They refer to body, sensory, and/or spatial experiences (e.g. I want to *get over* my disappointment and *move on*. He has a lot of responsibilities to *shoulder*.)

enacting metaphors: the client physically gets up and moves through space. As they step into the space a symbol occupies, they may experience that symbol's emotions; they can try out the role or actions of that symbol; they perceive from that symbol's perspective.

Explanations: the stories and analyses a client offers about the who, what, why, and so forth of their situation and themselves. They may or may not be accurate or relevant; they may reveal patterns and processes. Explanations are statements of fact.

gestural metaphors: metaphors suggested by body movements.

"invitation to metaphor": the facilitator asks a Clean Language question that asks for a metaphor for a feeling, gesture, experience, and so forth that a client introduces (e.g. And that's *like* what?). Usually sought for a resource or Desired Outcome.

"logic of the landscape": refers to the idiosyncratic characteristics of a client's metaphors and their interactions. Each client's landscape of metaphors has its own rules and processes, which may or may not coincide with our daily, earthly logic (e.g. If a heart is surrounded in ice, heat may melt the ice... or simple awareness of the ice could melt it, or a vibration.)

internalized metaphors: largely subconscious metaphors that encode a client's experiences and their interpretations of them.

latent resource: a resource whose value is not readily apparent to the client. Its usefulness may only become apparent at a later time.

looping: a return to a previous stage in the modeling process (e.g. a client may determine a desired outcome only to come back to the same or another problem or remedy). Also refers to a client's movement back and forth among the five stages of the Symbolic Modeling process, rather than moving sequentially from Stage 1-5.

maturing: Stage 5 of the Symbolic Modeling process involves the exploration of the effects of a change (1) in the moment (2) on the already-existing landscape, (3) as the client moves forward in time in the new landscape, extending the influence of and concretizing the change.

metaphor: a comparison of two unlike things that share one or more qualities or characteristics; a description of one thing or experience in terms of another. In Clean Language, the term encompasses parables, similes, analogies, and the like.

metaphor landscape: the sum total of a client's symbolic images as they relate to one another.

metaphor map: a client's depiction of their metaphors as they relate spatially to one another, like locations on a map.

modeling: the process of developing a model of the client's internal world, which may include their internalized metaphors. Modeling entails using a variety of strategies to help a client discover more about themselves, their symbols, and their interactive relationships and pattern.

natural trance: A hypnotic state induced by conversational guidance (as compared to a formal, scripted induction). A deeply self-reflective state; a state of mindful inner focus with easier access to the subconscious.

neuroplasticity: the brain's capacity to be flexible, to change, to grow new neurons and new connections between neurons.

overt metaphor: the comparison of a person, place, or thing to another is quite obvious (ex. Our negotiations have reached a dead end).

overt resource: a resource whose value is immediately evident.

physicalizing metaphors: refers to putting a metaphor into some kind of physical form (e.g. a drawing or clay model).

remedy: a client's desire to have less of something; the statement includes both their problem and their want; what will result from a remedy is not clear.

REPROCess: acronym for Resource, Explanation, Problem, Remedy, Outcome, Change and -ess for reprocessing itself.

reviewing: the facilitator verbally repeats multiple words and images to help the client keep a large piece of their metaphor landscape in their conscious awareness, generally in anticipation of asking a question about it all or to bring closure to a session.

resource: that which a client identifies as being helpful or of some value to them. It could be a tool, person, skill, knowledge, place, feeling, or attitude, for example.

resource state: a *feeling* or *state of being* that, once achieved, will help a client do what they want to do or change what they need to change.

resource symbol: a symbol or metaphor that is helpful to a client in some way.

self-modeling: when a client explores their inner world for themselves, discovering new information about its elements and/or metaphors and their relationships and patterns.

scope of practice: refers to the appropriate clients and issues that a professional facilitator should take on, given their training, experience, and the contract of services to be provided.

specialized questions: Clean Language questions in addition to the basic 12 that are commonly used in SyM. May also be created by the facilitator following the fundamental CL requirements: they need to be simple, clean, and true to the logic of the client's landscape.

symbolic domain: A client is described as being "in the/their symbolic domain" when they are in an inner-focused, mindful state, *exploring and experiencing their internalized metaphors*. We say they "leave the symbolic domain" when they return to an alert, fully conscious awareness of their surroundings; they are no longer in touch with their metaphors in an *experiential* way.

Symbolic Modeling: a language-based, mind/body process that invites a client to achieve greater clarity about any personal topic, including themselves, and to work through problematic issues at a very deep level. It uses three elements: Clean Language, metaphors, and modeling.

systems thinking: approaching a whole (such as a person or organization) as an interactive system of parts. In linear thinking, the emphasis is on how one part influences another part (cause and effect). Systems thinking pays particular attention to the feedback the effecting part gets from the affected parts, and how it responds in turn.

to-be-converted resource: a symbol or state of being that initially appears to be problematic or threatening but has the potential to become useful (ex. anger that "burns" in a client's belly becomes the fuel that motivates them to make a desired change.)

top-down approach/technique: a counseling or coaching strategy based on a model that has established categories, types, or scripted exercises. The counselor or coach determines how to work with the client based on a theory as to what best suits that type of client or situation (ex. Myers-Briggs Inventory, NLP [neuro-linguistic programming], Enneagrams).

MINING YOUR METAPHORS

Change the metaphor, Change the Self

Gina Campbell, Director and Trainer

visit **www.cleanlanguageresources.com**
and keep up to date on what's happening!

Sign up for our newsletter and learn about the latest...

Training opportunities
Online courses
New publications
Clean applications

...and more

Join Mining Your Metaphors on...

Facebook
and
LinkedIn

...for links to articles of interest.

Using this workbook to teach others? Request a free copy of

The Trainer's Guide to How-To Workbooks on Clean Language and Symbolic Modeling Parts I and II

Send an email to
gina@cleanlanguageresources.com

Printed in the United States
by Baker & Taylor Publisher Services